Innovation

Why, What and How

Innovation

Why, What and How

Sanjiv Narang

Vitasta

Let Knowledge Spread

Published by
Renu Kaul Verma
Vitasta Publishing Pvt Ltd
2/15, Ansari Road, Daryaganj
New Delhi - 110 002
info@vitastapublishing.com

ISBN 978-93-82711-32-2

First Edition 2016
2nd Reprint 2023

MRP ₹299

Typeset by Vits Press
Printed by Vikas Computer and Printers

Dedication

To my parents who encouraged me to challenge the status quo and create new concepts;
To my teachers of English and Math who taught me to be creative with precision;
To my organisational clients who gave me the opportunity to work in the domain of innovation.

Contents

Acknowledgements

I acknowledge the tacit contribution of all the participants of my training programmes on, 'Innovation' because in the process of facilitating these programmes and innovation projects,new insights regarding innovation emerged. The contribution of Renu Kaul Verma, the publisher, is significant because she agreed to publish this book after reading a few chapters . That was a high point. I also wish to acknowledge the valuable suggestions given by editors Tina Jindal and Papri Sri Raman in the process of rectifying errors and giving the final shape to this book.

Author's Note

There is a crying need prevalent almost everywhere i see,
The crying need to be saved from endemic problems,
The crying need to do more than we can,
The crying need for justice,
The crying need for solutions to seemingly insurmountable problems,
The crying need to be something more than an insignificant microscopic organism,
This crying need remains unaddressed because of our inability to innovate and evolve.

Preface

A common misconception in social circles is that innovation pertains only to technical areas. This misconception has resulted in our inability to think creatively and go beyond our knowledge boundaries in our domains of expertise. In fact, innovation is a dynamic phenomenon which can occur in any field of human endeavour. Whenever we are able to create new insights and go beyond the boundaries of the existing knowledge base, we enter the realm of innovation.

This book contains practical tools of innovation and the innovation development process.

It builds in a high degree of practical learning which has been consolidated over a period of one and a half decades in the process of analysing and synthesising the innovation development processes.

The Innovation Tools and Levers are a result of experiential learning and insights gathered during my work across industrial boundaries.

The repeated application of Innovation Tools and their subsequent redesigning has resulted in their becoming increasingly 'user friendly'.

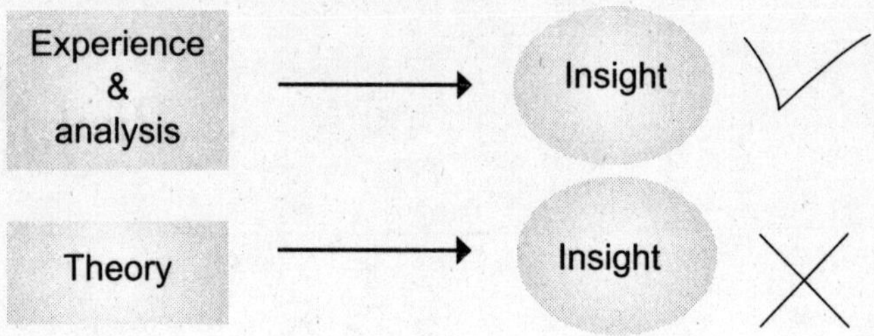

These tools can be used to generate innovations in functional and key performance areas.

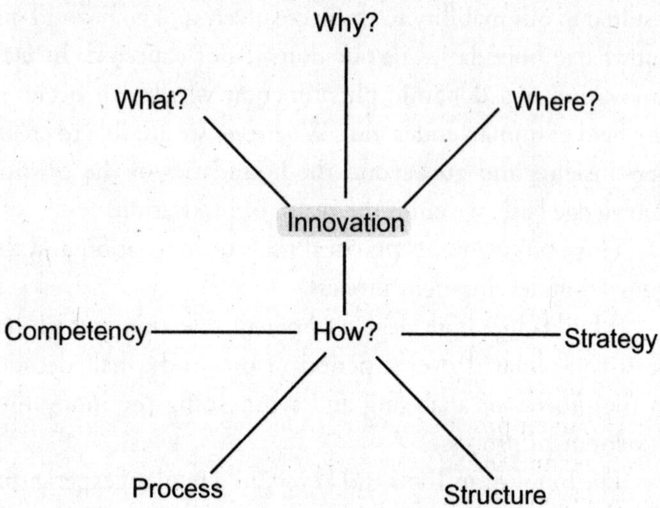

How to become an Innovator?

This is a question that plagues those individuals who do not want to be a part of the crowd; anyone who wants to be a pioneer; anyone who aspires for greatness; and anyone who wants to change the world.

It is a question that plagues organisations that desire to generate innovation after innovation, but fail repeatedly in the process.

It is also a question that arises when we see institutions in a state of dilapidation and decline.

It is nothing but a question that plagues individuals who are stuck in situations, which seemingly cannot be resolved.

We will answer this question and map the path on which an innovator has to travel in order to achieve targets that no one has achieved before.

Our approach would include answering the following fundamental questions:

Innovation: Why?

Most professionals would spend their professional life in following the practices learnt.

In fact most professionals unconsciously feel that their key objective is to implement what they have learnt; and they tend to be on a morally higher plane as they are implementing the set standards with diligence. They unconsciously believe that implementation of learnt knowledge is the sine-qua-non of professional competence.

The consequence of this style of thinking is that they start and end their careers by being followers, creating hardly a ripple in their professions. They disappear without a trace.

Innovation is necessary for visibility. However, it is not an easy task to accomplish. A ready-made innovative solution mapped in a book is not available. There is no teacher who can hold your hand and show the right path. It involves venturing into the unknown. Risk is embedded in it. It is like walking on broken glass. So why should one aspire to be an innovator in one's chosen profession? This is a critical question that will be answered in the first chapter of this book.

This question we shall examine from the angles of the importance of innovation for:

- Organisations
- Countries
- Civilisations
- Economy
- Leaders

Innovation: What?

The term innovation is usually understood to mean, 'Product Innovation'. This is a broad interpretation of the term. The meaning of the term has evolved with the appearance of innovation in every professional domain. Thus, whatever profession one chooses to follow, one can innovate and be an innovator in that area.

A comprehensive perspective regarding innovation and its manifestations evolves in the second chapter of this book.

Innovation: How?

Now we come to the mother of all questions, 'How to innovate?'

We shall examine the different tools of innovation and the process of applying them. This is the major question that will occupy us in this book. Each tool has its own power. However, the tools will not compensate for the absence of passion, which is a critical ingredient in the making of an innovator.

We shall explore and apply the concepts *of'Competency* of innovation' and '*The process of developing innovations*'.

Innovation: Where?

Where to start? Where to apply the competency of innovation? Where would an innovation have the maximum impact? Where would the 'Return on Investment' in terms of effort and resources be the maximum?

In a nut shell, what should be the '*Innovation Strategy*'?

We shall examine this question in the chapter '*Innovation Hotspots*'.

How to patent an innovation?

Patenting of innovation enables the innovator to protect his/her intellectual property and benefit from it. The system of patenting enables the innovator to get the requisite return on investment of time, effort and resources that he has put in, in order to generate the innovation. However, patenting is only possible in reference to products and processes.

How to enhance the innovation level in an organisation?

Organisations make numerous efforts to innovate in their key result areas. These efforts are high profile initially. However, they tend to lose steam and are quickly confined to the dustbins of organisational history that no one wants to re-examine or even touch.

How can an organisation make these interventions successful? What should an organisation do so that the culture of innovation develops? What should it do so that it churns out innovation after innovation by continuously renewing itself? We shall answer these questions in the chapter, '*Innovation Ecosystem*'.

What have I got to do with innovation?

How do I innovate?

Why should I innovate?

Where do I innovate?

How do I benefit from innovation?

How do I protect my intellectual property?

How do I raise the level of innovation in my organisation?

How do I design an innovation ecosystem?

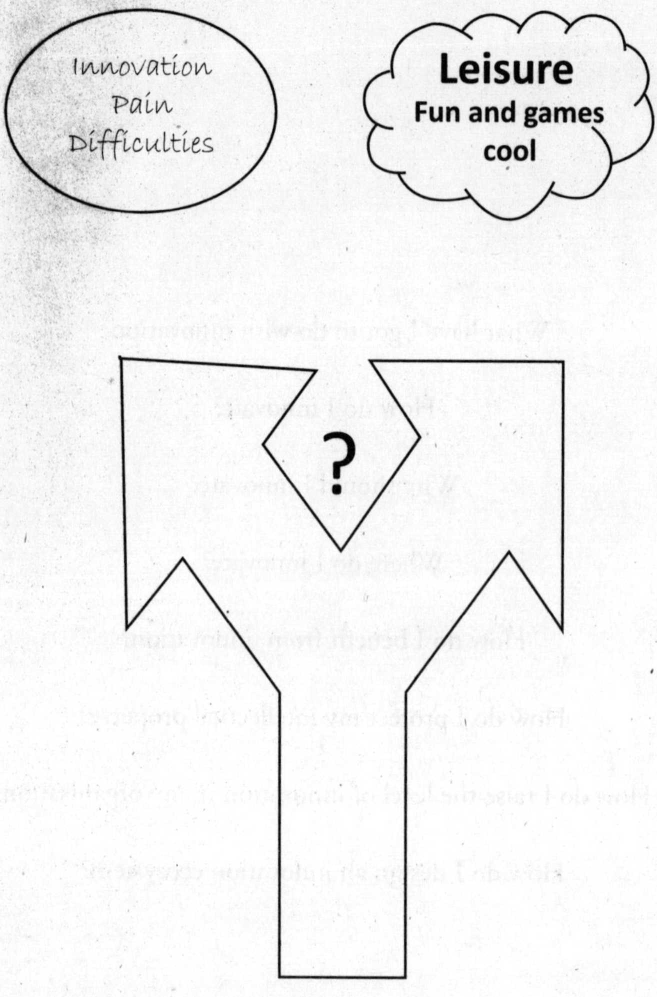
Innovation
Pain
Difficulties
Leisure
Fun and games
cool
?

Innovation: Why?

Imagine the nomadic man, standing on the top of a hill, with a basket of fruits. His legs ache because he has made many trips to the top of the hill to carry fruits down to the base of the hill. He sees some logs nearby. He puts them together, keeps his basket on top of them and rolls them down the hill. The logs roll for some distance and then the 'basket of fruits' fall off.

Idea failure! Dejection! Weariness engulfs the nomadic man.

Was the idea a failure ?

No.

The idea was the seed of a subsequent innovation called **the 'Wheel'** which became fundamental to the locomotion of humanity.

Hence, the whole brain thinking skills of creativity and analytical capability constitute the seed of innovation.

The above innovation pattern has replicated itself continuously to enable the "growth of humankind", resulting in its ability to fly through the air; subjugate almost all animals; go to the moon; live in large social groups called 'countries' and so on. Looking at innovation from another angle, we observe that innovation has a positive correlation with economic, organisational as well as personal growth. In fact key innovations serve as milestones for the evolution of human kind.

In most organisations, innovation is like a spark, which is more or less quickly extinguished. Unexamined repetition without any improvement prevails. This is fast becoming a prescription for suicide in the currently crowded market scenario.

The current economic and competitive environment dictates that without innovation an organisation can not even enter the market. Therefore, it follows that for any kind of growth-whether for market share or profit-Innovation is imperative. Experimentation precedes innovation. Since experimentation is not limited to the R & D department only, creation of ideas is possible at any operational point in the organisation. Hence, innovation is possible in each and every vertical of the organisation, whether it is the HR, IT, Training, Performance management, Marketing, Operations, Sales, or even the Treasury department.

Taking cognisance of the link of innovation to humankind's survival and growth, it is quite surprising that the focus on this critical aspect is rather limited.

In the universe everything is in a state of flux. A system starts deteriorating as soon as it goes into equilibrium. Therefore, if we don't innovate, we are bound to decline.

Innovating is extraordinarily tough. So why should one

aspire towards innovation?

Is it worth it?

Unless we have a complete and undying belief in the power and utility of innovation there is no point in trying to attempt it and leaving the work undone half way.

So, lets examine the utility of innovation towards:

- Organisations
- Countries
- Entrepreneurship
- Leadership
- Customers
- Economy

1. Organisations

Why do organisations embark on the path of innovation? What value do they derive by doing so?

Quite frankly, without innovation organisations decline and eventually die. Let us take a look at some case histories to clarify understanding of the dynamics unleashed by innovation, or the lack of it.

Leading Case: HMT

Facts: When I was in class X, I did a project for my economics paper. The organisation that I chose was HMT. I distinctly remember that HMT was the leading watch manufacturer in India at that time. It had the maximum market share and also had technological superiority over its competitors.

What is the status of HMT today?

It is a dying organisation.

Questions

- What happened?
- How could it decline so rapidly?
- What was the critical cause of its decline?

Analysis

- Competitors like Titan innovated while HMT stagnated.
- Titan came up with innovations in Products, Processes such as the New Product Development Process, Marketing and Sales.
- The impact of such innovations is visible in the profitability figures of Titan, its brand equity and its dominant market share.
- Thus, Titan is able to hold on to its market share in spite of stiff competition from almost all international brands.

Conclusion

- Innovation leads to growth while the lack of it leads to decline.
- Innovation is a multi-pronged phenomenon that is not limited to product innovation only. It extends to process innovation, sales innovation as well as marketing innovation.

Leading Case: ICICI Bank

Facts: ICICI Bank started operations in India as a bank in 1994. It has grown into the second largest bank in India. It is also the largest private sector bank in India. On comparing it with SBI (State Bank of India), we find a startling difference as shown below, although SBI started operations as Bank of Calcutta in 1806.

Net ProfitMargin(%)	2011	2012	2013	2014	2015
ICICI Bank	20.3	20.1	21.4	22.3	22.3
SBI	9.4	10.4	10.7	7.5	8.2

Question

- Why has ICICI grown at a much faster pace in comparison to SBI?

Analysis

- ICICI has actively pursued and deployed innovation focused on technology and customer requirements.
  Example: 3-in-1 account (Product Innovation):
  ICICI was the fastest in accounts innovation. It was the first Indian bank to launch an online share trading as well as demat account, combined together. It launched the 3-in-1 account in 1997 consisting of a savings account, a demat account and an online trading account.

ATMs

- ICICI was the fastest bank in this area too.

Banking at any branch

- This was a heretofore new experience for the Indian customer. Even if one had a savings account in New Delhi, one could operate it from Pathankot.

Customer focused innovation

- ICICI bank redesigned its branches and made them more

customer friendly. The banking environment of the branch was more hospitable. The tellers spoke decently to the customers and the customers had a decent place to sit while waiting for their drafts.

Conclusion

- Product innovation, process innovation and customer focused innovations have a direct impact on the top and the bottom line of any organisation.

Leading Case: Havell's India

Facts: A ceiling fan in my house got burnt. It was expensive to get it repaired. So I decided to purchase a new fan. When I inquired about the prices, I found that Havell's fans were priced at Rs 1,400 while the other fans were priced at Rs 1,000.

Question

Why are Havell's fans priced at a premium price and are still the preferred buys?

Analysis

- Havell's fans use 50 Watts of electric power while the other fans utilise 75 Watts.
- Havell's fans are designed to enhance the span of air circulation by 25%.

Conclusion

- Product innovation results in premium pricing.

Leading Case: Walmart

Facts: Walmart started its first store in the year 1962. In 2010 its sales were 405 billion USD.

Question

Why has Walmart grown at such an exponential pace while at the same time, its competitors have stagnated or even declined?

Analysis

The innovations implemented by Walmart are as follows:

Process Innovations

- Electronic cash registers
- Private satellite communication system
- Data warehousing
- Electronic data interchange
- RFID (Radio Frequency Identification)
- Online stores

Product Innovations

- Walmart set up large stores in rural areas which were full of small mom and pop stores.

  This combination of product and process innovations gave Walmart unique competitive advantages.

2. Countries

There is a direct correlation between the GDP of countries and the extent of innovation prevalent in them. The top countries of the world in terms of Patent Filings in 2015 as per World Intellectual Property Organization(WIPO) are :

Country	Rank
USA	1
Japan	2
China	3
Germany	4
Republic of Korea	5
France	6
U.K.	7

What is the pattern that emerges? These countries are characterized by robust and low cost economies coupled with high standard of living. These countries are also internationally powerful and exercise world hegemony.

Is there a link to their capacity to innovate?

The correlation is obvious.

Innovation metrics are the leading indicators of economic growth and development.

No country or organisation exists in a state of equilibrium. It either grows or declines in direct correlation with the level of innovation it institutes or creates.

Conclusion

- A combination of product and process innovation creates unique competitive advantages.
- No innovation lasts for a life-time. A continuous stream of innovation is required to create and sustain a competitive advantage.
- Process and product innovation collectively result in business model innovation.
- Innovation results in rapid growth.

3. Entrepreneurship

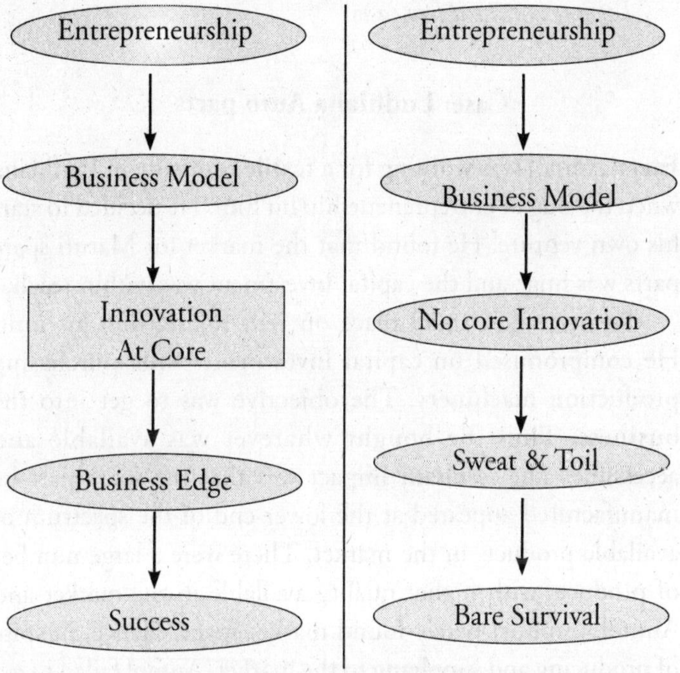

Is there a link between innovation and successful entrepreneurship?

Many individuals dream of creating a successful organisation or business, and 99% of the time the dream dies because the entrepreneur gets tired of the responsibility of running the show and trying to make the strings of income and expenditure meet.

It is quite painful to hear about broken dreams and unfulfilled visions.

What is the prime reason for their failure? Is there a link to lack of innovation in the business model of the organisation?

Let us examine a few cases:

Case: Ludhiana Auto parts

Facts: Anmol was working for a textile company in Ludhiana when the bug of entrepreneurship bit him. He decided to start his own venture. He found that the market for Maruti spare parts was huge and the capital investment was within reach.

So he took a small place on rent for starting his unit. He compromised on capital investment while purchasing production machinery. The objective was to get into the business. Thus, he bought whatever was available and accessible. The resultant impact was that the spare part he manufactured appeared at the lower end of the spectrum of available products in the market. There were a large number of products with higher quality available in the market and Anmol's product barely found market space. Hence, in spite of producing and supplying to the market, Anmol failed to get a return on his investment. He went out of business almost as fast as he started it.

Analysis:Starting an entrepreneurial business without a' Unique selling proposition' is a prescription for harakiri.

The USP of a business is dependent upon innovation in its core business model. Thus, starting a business without a significant product,process or business model innovation is a royal road to disaster.

Conclusion

Entrepreneurship without inherent innovation in product/

process/strategy or business model leads to subsequent failure.

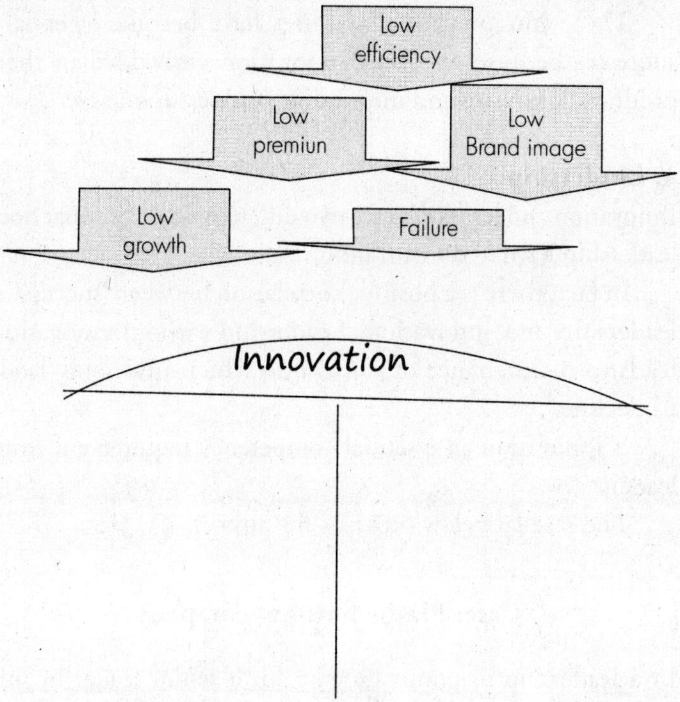

Now let us look at some entrepreneurial ventures which became astonishing successes:

- Microsoft
- Apple
- Venrock United Healthcare
- Cisco
- Hotmail
- Amazon.com

- Google
- Skype

These entrepreneurial ventures have become legendary successes because of steady innovation embedded in their products, processes and innovation Business models.

4. Leadership

Innovation and leadership are two different skills. So what does leadership have to do with innovation?

In fact, there is a positive correlation between 'successful leadership' and 'innovation'. Leadership without innovation leads to maintenance of status quo which invariably leads to decline.

Is innovation an essential competency requirement from leaders?

The case-let below provides the answer.

Case: Plastic bottling company

In a leadership diagnosis exercise for a senior leader in this company, one of the leadership competency gaps identified was that of 'innovation' The specific skill gaps that were identified are as follows:

- Technology trends
- Process innovation at the shop floor
- New management tools
- New product development

This indicates that innovation is a competency that is also expected from the leaders.

When a leader is selected to head an organization, what is the key agenda?

The leader needs to take the organization from Level A to Level B.

How is that going to be possible without innovation?

5.Customers

Innovation creates customer value.

Case: CIPLA

Cancer Treatment Drug	ERLOCIP	Competing Drug
Tablet(Each)	Rs.1,600.00	Rs.4,800.00
One Month's dose	Rs.46,000.00	Rs.1.4 lakhs

Therefore, why innovation?

Innovation for creating more customer value. In the aforementioned case,there is a 300 % increase in customer value because the price of a life essential drug has been reduced to one third of the competing drug. Thus,the product becomes within reach of atleast some of the patients when it was previously beyond their purchasing power.

6. Economy

Is there a possible link of the level of innovation in an economy and its being a low cost or a high cost economy?

Case: Horizontal drilling

It was not too long ago when the price per barrel of Brent crude was 118 dollars per barrel. Now the price per barrel of Brent crude is 42 dollars.
How has this happened?
Is there a link with innovation somewhere?

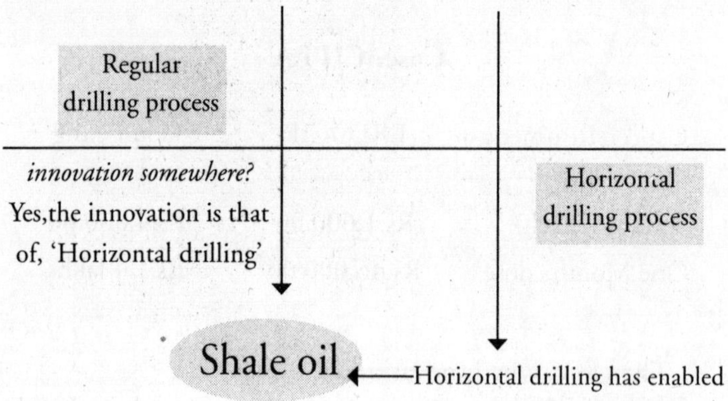

access to shale oil which was heretofore very expensive because of the high cost of drilling for shale oil.

Thus,innovation has the capacity to impact the core engine of an economy.

A high level of innovation translates into a low cost economy and a low level of innovation converts into a high cost economy.

Why Innovation?

Innovation for growth
Innovation for success
Innovation for survival
Innovation for solving saturated problems
Innovation for making a visible difference
Innovation for transformation
Innovation for reducing risk
Innovation for successful leadership
Innovation for a low cost economy

Innovation: What?

What are we referring to when we use the term 'innovation' or when we think about innovation?

What does innovation mean? What is the dominant perspective of innovation?

The meaning and understanding of innovation as an entity has changed over the decades. There was a time when it referred to only product innovation. Subsequently, process innovation became a part of it. However, now, the term innovation has broken into new vistas of thought and action.

Hence, the prevailing mindset related to innovation requires an immediate update

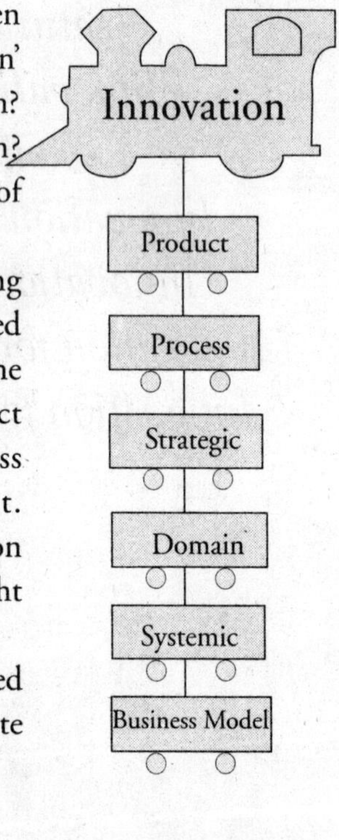

Product	Process	System
Strategy	Domain	Business Model

Product Innovation

This is the most visible form of innovation. Product innovations exist all around us. Any product that exists in the market today was an innovative idea sometime in history.. Some examples which epitomise product innovation are:

1. Bloom box

The bloom box is an electricity server which converts chemical energy into electrical energy without any combustion and the outpouring of harmful gases. It is an innovation created by Bloom Energy, and its popularity is such that a host of innovative companies like Google and Apple are also using it to power their electricity needs.

A bloom box, the size of a small cupboard is sufficient to power an average home for 2 years.

This product innovation has the potential of becoming a pioneering idea for the power producing industry.

There will be no need for huge power plants at the pit head of coal mines, and the huge power grid that is required to transport the generated electricity from remote power plants to urban areas could also become obsolete.

2. Tweel

Any individual who drives a vehicle knows the vagaries of a punctured tyre. How many times have you felt frustrated that you couldn't make it to an important meeting because of a flat tire?

A product innovation called the Tweel promises to eliminate the phenomenon of punctured tyres for ever.

Michelin, a tyre manufacturing organisation has designed a 'tyre without air'.

All the tyres which are in use are pneumatic tyres; they use air for inflating the tyre, thereby cushioning the drive.

Tweel designed by Michelin consists of a wheel made of polyurethane spokes, which—because of their design and elasticity—provide a cushioning impact which is very similar to that provided by air in pneumatic tyres.

If this innovation succeeds, it shall transform the tyre industry for ever and the fundamental model of a wheel will go through a miraculous change.

Process Innovation

Process innovation has always been the second wheel among different types of innovation. It does not have the same visibility associated with product innovation. However, in its ability to create value for the organisation as well as its stakeholders, it stands shoulder to shoulder with product innovation.

The lack of visibility of process innovation in terms of it

not having any defined physical shape is a roadblock in it being appreciated at par with product innovation.

The result of this lack of focus on process innovation is that organisations now hold dinosaurian processes close to their bosoms almost as if they were holy. This has resulted in a wave of inefficiency creeping into the working systems and the innards of organisations. However, this inefficiency remains hidden because processes are invisible entities. One feels its impact but one is not able to grasp it and resolve it because there is no organisational focus on process innovation. It is nobody's responsibility.An organisation is a sum total of work processes, both defined and undefined.

Any improvement in a work process has a cascading impact on all the downstream processes thereby enhancing overall organisational effectiveness and efficiency.

Measurement of the effectiveness of a process:

The effectiveness of a process is measured on the basis of four parameters:

- Quality
- Quantity
- Cost
- Time

Any process innovation can be called an innovation only if there is an improvement on any or all of these parameters.

This also reflects the cascading impact of process innovation on Quality, Quantity, Cost and Time, which are critical parameters for making any organisation successful.

Case: Process Innovation

Process name: Mobile phone documentation process Process description:When one purchases a SIM card from a retailer of a telecom company there are certain documents that need to be submitted to the retailer. The process followed by the submitted documents is mapped below:

Process Map:

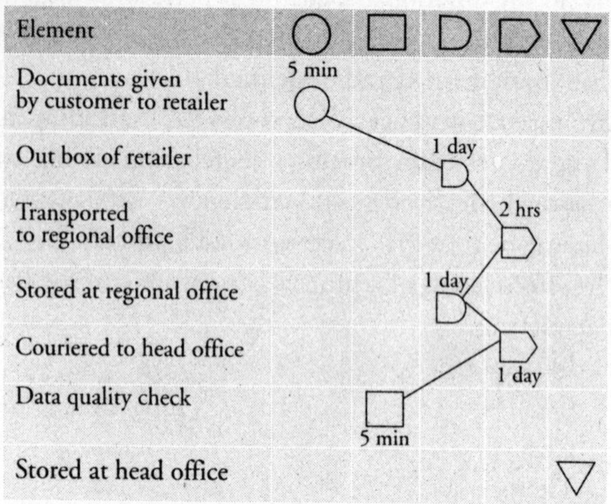

Turn Around Time (TAT)=3 days 2 hrs and 10 mins

Symbols used in the process map

These are symbols used in Industrial engineering. Hence they are employed worldwide for process mapping.

The utilisation of these symbols is essential for "Process Mapping". However, they have not found their way into the lexicon of a modern manager because they are categorised under

Industrial engineering, which is an esoteric subject and hence only available to those who have a panache for mathematics.

Symbol	Meaning
○	Operation
□	Inspection
⇨	Transport
D	Delay
▽	Storage

Nothing can be further away from the actual state of affairs. Process mapping is a simple skill and since every manager is first and foremost the manager of work processes, it is a vital skill for effective management.

System Innovation A system consists of multiple processes which interact with one another to convert an input into an output. For example, Judicial System, Production System, Sales System and Accounting system. This shows that systemic innovation is a higher order skill in comparison to process innovation. In systemic innovation we are required to think at the system's level rather than at the process level. It would invariably involve multiple process innovations.

The skill of process mapping enables us to see the process, thereby enabling the visibility of the underlying inadequacies, errors and wastage.

Wastage visible in the above Process Map

- Unnecessary delay of 3 days, when the documents are

waiting to be transported or processed.

- Unnecessary physical transportation which is not only time consuming but also cost ineffective.
- High (Turn around time) may result in call barring, thereby creating revenue loss for the organisation.

Process Innovation Example:A process innovation which removes the above inadequacies of the existing process is mapped below:

S.No	Element	○	□	D	⇨	▽
1	Documents given by Customer to retailer	○ 5 min				
2	Document scanning by retailer using document scanner given by the organisation	○ 15 min				
3	E-mailed to H.O. server	○ 15 min				
4	Stored at H.O.					▽

TAT= 35 mins.

*Analysis and conclusion:*The power of process innovation is visible in the above case. The TAT has been reduced from 3 days 2 hrs and 10 mins to 35 mins. Thus, we are not only saving significant time, but are also reducing the corresponding cost and enhancing the quality of output.

Such potential is rampant in most organisations. However, it remains untapped because of the competency gap of most managers in the area of process mapping and process innovation. The over all impact of living with inadequate processes is high cost of living, thereby resulting in the phenomenon of everybody working very hard but still only getting enough for basic survival.

Strategic Innovation

Strategic innovation has always had a major impact on outcomes in the annals of history. During world war II, various types of strategic innovations were tried by both the German army as well as the allied forces. Some of these were grand successes while others were colossal failures.

The 'Bridge too far' strategy adopted by the allied forces to capture the bridges, so that the movement of the allied tanks is not hampered was one such strategic innovation. It only had partial success and there was a tremendous loss of life.

Apple's change of strategic direction from computers to mobiles is an example of strategic innovation, which turned out to be a phenomenal success. The move by Infosys from Software services to Software consulting was a kind of "Strategic Innovation".

The key learning point in these examples is that a strategic innovation tends to succeed only when all the components of the strategic innovation have been put into place. Even if one component ceases to be potent, the entire innovation can collapse like a house of cards. The same lesson resonates through and through the annals of history. The introduction of a mouse infected with plague in the camp of the Greek army, so as to trigger their withdrawal is another example of a strategic innovation that was a phenomenal success.

Domain Innovation

Domain innovation refers to the scope of innovation in every field of human endeavour. Whatever be your area of work, you can always create something new in it.

Basically, everyone has a choice. You could either spend your entire lifetime doing what has already been laid out, or you could challenge the existing knowledge base thereby creating novel ideas and new possibilities.

Since nothing is perfect and everything is in a state of evolution, the possibility of being creative is infinite. The challenge, however, lies in converting this creativity into workable innovations.

Thus, when a leader thinks of a new system of communicating with the people, it is a domain innovation; when an HRD professional deploys a new Organization Development (OD) intervention, it is a domain innovation; when a sales professional designs a new system of display for the customer, it is a domain innovation; when Rowling writes a new story titled 'Harry Potter', it is domain innovation; and when the personality of James Bond goes through a critical redesign from indefatigable to vulnerable in,'Skyfall', it is domain innovation.

Case: Domain Innovations in HR

- Strategic HR
- Competency mapping
- HR analytics

Case: Harry Potter-Domain innovation in writing

The author created a completely new concept in the form of a world of magic complete with its ministry of magic, magical sports, politics in the world of magic, values in the world of magic and a school in the world of magic. This is a classic example of domain innovation that we see repeated in other great classics such as "Lord of the Rings" or "The Shiva Trilogy" as well.

Case: James Bond in Skyfall—Domain innovation in characterisation

James Bond is traditionally depicted as an invincible individual who can beat insurmountable odds, repeatedly. However in Skyfall, James Bond is depicted as a person who can lose, get beaten up, is vulnerable and is developing a white stubble, i.e. not young anymore.

Business Model Innovation

Business model innovation is more comprehensive in comparison to the other forms of innovation cited so far. It is a combination of multiple types of innovation. For example, when an organisation implements product as well as strategic innovation, it becomes a business model innovation.

The business model focuses on strategy, process and product. Even if two of these innovations are triggered together in an organisation, business model innovation ensues.

Case: Titan

Titan focused on strategic innovation by examining new geographical markets for its products. In addition, it also catalyzed innovation in new product development as well as process innovation in terms of the new product development process. This was accompanied by 'Innovation in Sales' which consisted of selling watches in showrooms.

These simultaneous innovations in strategy, process and product department fall under the category of 'Business Model Innovation'. Business model innovation is crucial for entrepreneurs. Without this vertical of innovation any entrepreneurial venture is bound to fail. Even if it survives, it will aspire to consume all the available resources and will still

Innovation: How?

barely survive.

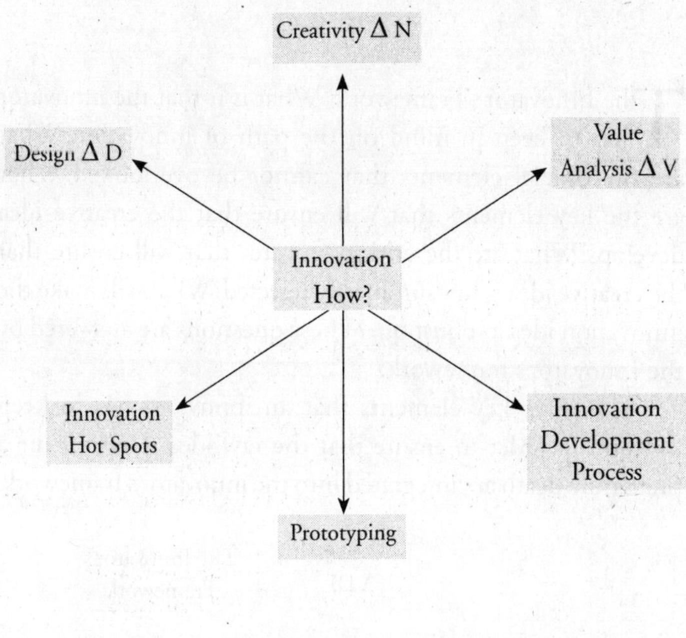

The innovator's framework

The Innovator's Framework. What is it that the innovator has to keep in mind on the path of innovation?What are the crucial elements that cannot be overlooked?What are the key elements that will ensure that the creative idea develops?What are the critical features that will ensure that the creative idea is not summarily rejected?What will make the innovation idea a robust one?These questions are answered by the Innovator's framework.

The three key elements that an innovator has to keep in mind in order to ensure that the raw idea does not die a premature death are integrated into the innovator's framework.

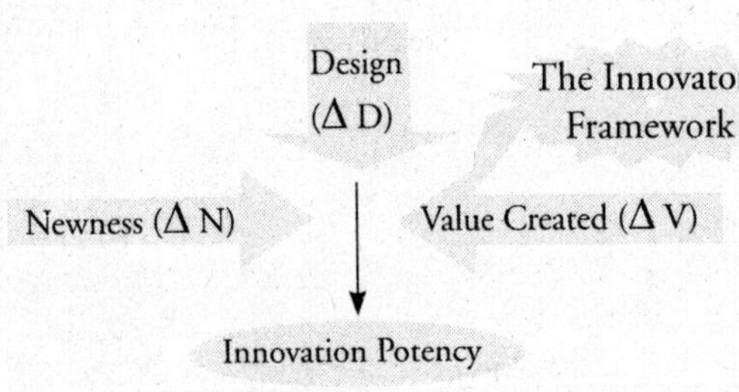

These elements are delineated below

1. New mental pattern (Δ N)

This is the starting point of the creative process. The term "New" in this element is vital. The idea cannot be an extension of an existing or working idea. It has to be new or novel. There has to be some characteristic of the raw idea that is fundamentally different from what already exists.

The level of newness i.e. Δ N will determine whether the idea so generated will be considered to be innovative or not. If Δ N is low, then the idea is only an extension of an existing idea and thus, does not qualify as an innovation.

The crux of any creative process is Δ N, ie the generation of a new mental pattern or the generation of a new concept. If the new mental pattern is not consciously created, the old mental pattern continues to have a stranglehold on our mind. Our thinking remains imprisoned in the confines of the old mindset. If the mindset is not consciously changed, we remain prisoners of the old mindset throughout our lives. Hence, we could get locked in a cycle of endless repetition.

This creative process is not easy. It either requires an inspiring brainwave or disciplined application of innovation tools.Can we trigger brainwaves? Or do we have to wait for years for an inspiration to blossom? Unfortunately, the answer to these questions is an enigma, as a stroke of innovation may or may not come.

The utilisation of innovation tools enables us to get out of this conundrum.

When a new concept is formed, it is generally loose and not crystal clear. An unclear idea or a loose idea is liable to be rejected outright. Therefore, a raw idea has to be developed before it can be presented.

The formation of a new mental pattern is the first creative challenge in the quest for innovation. It seems easy but it isn't. The enormity of the challenge becomes visible only when we start trying. Then, it seems that the concerned product or process has everything that it could possibly have.

What else is possible?

The mind is blank and the answer does not pop out. This happens because the mind does not have an answer. The answer has to be created consciously through the application of creativity skills.

The re-designed mental pattern is called the New Mental Pattern (NMP).

2. Value creation (Δ V)

An innovation only becomes successful if it creates new value.

How is the new value created ?

New value is created by satisfying unsatisfied needs.

The range and depth of the needs satisfied indicate the value created by the innovation. Unless this value exceeds the value created by existing solutions, the designed solution cannot be defined as an innovation. Thus, the innovative solution needs to create new value in terms of either new needs satisfied or the satisfaction of prevalent needs at lesser cost.

Though 'needs' seem to be an easy enough concept to comprehend and utilise, it is a rather dynamic concept. Needs can be clubbed into the following categories:

- User needs:

  Range of needs

Indicating the number of needs of the user which are satisfied by the proposed solution.

Depth of needs

Indicating the level of satisfaction per user need.

- Process needs:

  Process inadequacies or process limitations.
- Needs of intermediaries:

  Unsatisfied needs of intermediaries between the user and the maker.
- Latent Needs:

  Needs of the user which the user himself doesn't know.

These needs will only surface when the solution gets utilised and the need is suddenly felt.

The range and depth of needs satisfied gives us the benefits of the innovation. Benefits divided by costs enables us to calculate Δ V.

The greater the range and depth of needs satisfied by the proposed innovative solution, the greater is the value of the proposed innovation and greater is the corresponding chance of its success.

How do we enhance Δ V? Either we enhance the benefits at the same level of costs to the user, or we maintain benefits and reduce costs. The third possibility which is a sure shot criteria of success is that we increase benefits and reduce costs.

That is the hallmark of innovation; increase in benefits accompanied by reduction in costs. If Δ V is significant, the third element of the innovator's framework comes into focus, i.e. Design.

3. Design (Δ D)

This element of the Innovator's Framework adds substance to the innovative idea.

It converts the fuzzy idea into a concrete idea with specifications and dimensions. This stage can also be called virtual prototyping.

This element of the innovator's framework initiates the 'hands-on' work of the innovator. This is when the innovator starts interacting with his creation. This is also when the first challenges of practicality are felt by the innovator. The design stage now would involve multiple iterations between the design, the new mental pattern and the needs satisfied.

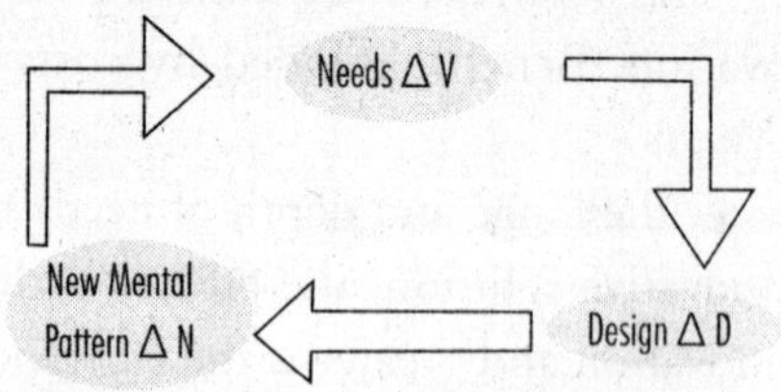

Without the design, presenting the raw idea to the critical stakeholders would amount to committing suicide.

For product innovation ideas, the design consists of 2D/3D design which is a diagrammatic representation of the innovation idea.

For process innovations, the design will consist of flow charting along with the designs of input and output formats for different stakeholders in the designed system. For new concepts, metaphoric infographs can be utilised.

The three components of the 'Innovator's Framework'

taken together constitute the 'Potent Innovation Idea'. Now the idea is developed and it is ready for presentation to the critical stakeholders so that the prototyping budget can be acquired.

Innovation Development Process

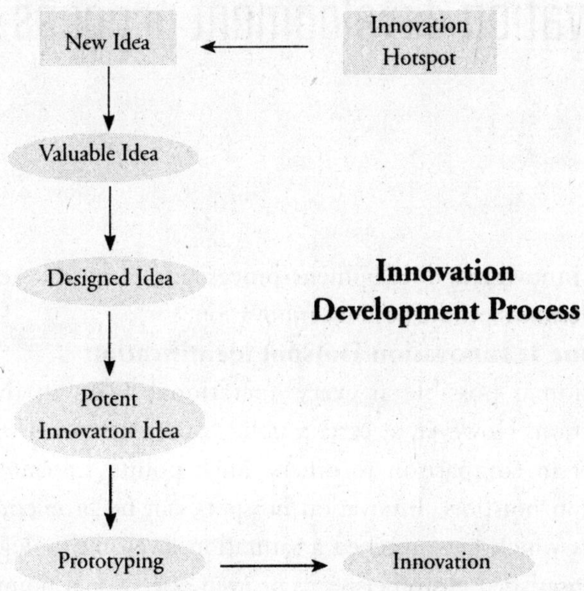

The innovation development process indicates the key milestones on the path of innovation.

Innovation development process?

The innovation development process indicates the key milestones on the path of innovation.

Milestone 1: Innovation Hotspot identification

Innovation is possible at every operational point in the organisation. However, at certain points the return on effort is higher in comparison to others. Such points are called innovation hotspots. Innovation hotspots can be problems, solutions which have reached a saturation level, technology shifts, unsatisfied customer needs or even operational points that add the maximum value in the value chain.

Milestone 2: Δ N (Newness)

This is the raw idea that is generated after due application of creativity tools or the unconscious creative process for catalysing the formation of new imagination or new mental patterns.

The end point of this element of the innovation development process is the existence of a raw idea that is new.

The creative idea may consist of multiple elements. Some of the elements may have been retained from the existing solutions and some may be extensions of existing idea elements, but some critical elements of the idea have to be predominantly new.

If the elements of newness are few and there is a domination of elements that have already been in existence, the innovator runs the risk of being received with the feedback—'That is not an innovation. We have tried that before'. A mere extension of existing ideas does not qualify as an innovation.

The level of newness, ie. Δ N, is the predominate factor which determines whether the entity created qualifies to be an innovation.

Milestone 3: Valuable Idea (Δ V)

Every new and creative idea that is generated is not a valuable idea. A creative idea may or may not be valuable.

What determines the value of an idea?

The value of an idea is determined by the range and depth of the needs that it satisfies. The needs of the user segments, the process needs and the needs of intermediaries. These constitute the benefits of the creative idea.

However, even the benefits of a creative idea are not equated to value. We have to examine the costs of the idea also.

Value = Benefits/Costs

$\Delta V = \Delta B / \Delta C$

This value analysis yields Δ V.

Δ V indicates the new value created i.e. the change in value. It specifies the value proposition of the creative idea. Δ V is the predominate factor that determines whether the innovation will succeed or fail.

Milestone 4: Designed Idea (Δ D)

The value of an idea brings to the fore the possible return on investment of time and money on the innovation project. If the value of a creative idea is insufficient or unsatisfactory, the innovator needs to go back and generate a more valuable idea. However, if the value of an idea is exciting and enticing, then the idea needs to be shaped in terms of design. A diagram of the idea with specifications is essential if the creative idea has to progress further on the innovation trail.

A 2D design is a minimum requirement, however, by using software such as Google sketch, 3D design models of the innovation idea is a possibility.

Milestone 5: Check Patents for Innovation Potency

A continual iteration among the design, the value and the newness of the idea enhances the potency of the concept. These three stages make the creative idea robust.

However, are they enough to determine innovation potency? No!

In order to determine innovation potency the innovator has to access the patent databases and compare the innovation concept generated with the patents that exist in the patent databases. If a similar patent already exists, the newness of the innovation concept disappears and thus the innovation concept generated loses its innovation potency. This step in the innovation development process is crucial because if this step is not executed in all its seriousness, the innovator may end up re-inventing the wheel or even inadvertently infringing a registered patent.

The innovation idea has innovation potency (Δ P) if there is significant Δ N, Δ V & Δ D w.r.t. the already existing patents in the patent databases.

$\Delta P = f(\Delta N, \Delta V, \Delta D)$ where Δ P = Innovation Potency

Δ N = Newness

Δ V=New value created
Δ D=New Design

Milestone 6: Prototyped Idea

Prototyping is the final denouement of the interaction of concept and reality. The creative idea has to finally take its real form. The formulation of a working model acts as a "Proof of concept" and thus is essential to demonstrate the utility of the potent innovation idea.

Multiple prototypes need to be developed and tested before the innovator is ready to roll out the innovation.

What is the utility of following this innovation development process?

The utility of following this innovation development process is reduced probability of costly mistakes happening on the path of innovation.

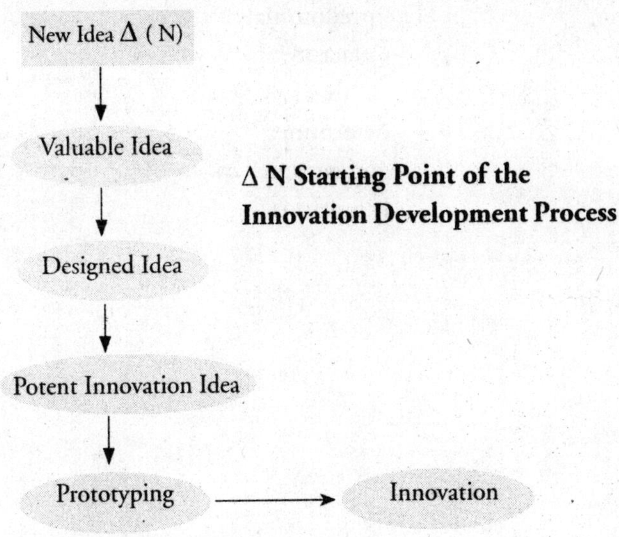

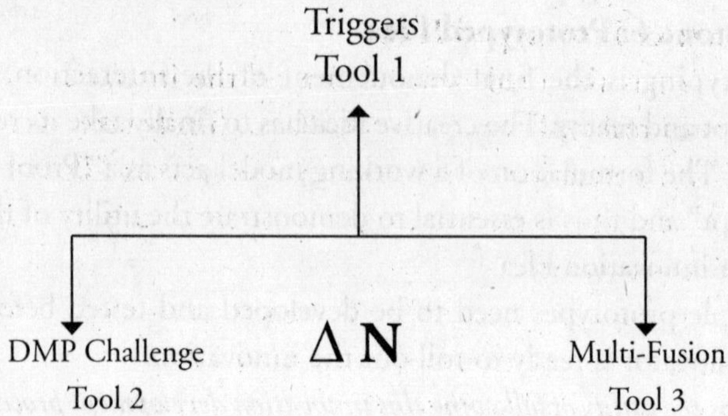

Δ N

The predominant
factor
that
determines
Categorization as an
Innovation

Triggers (Δ N Tool 1)

Over a period of time, creativity has become such a bandied about term that the underlying skill has become mired in magic. Thus skill development in the field of creativity has either not been tried or it has been blocked by the misplaced belief that creativity is inborn and thus cannot be enhanced.

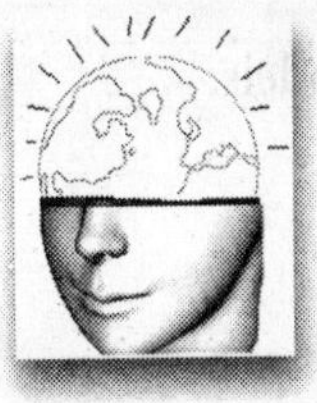

When we set out on the journey of creativity, the starting point is the focus. The focus of creativity can be any entity under the sun. The more central the focus area to the process of value creation, more would be the realisation of the creative effort. It can be a product, a process, a concept or a service. Let's take an example of a creativity focus—the training room.

Creativity Focus: Training Room

Dominant Mental Pattern

The DMP is the first response of the brain to the stimulus 'Training Room'. It assimilates our earlier experience of training rooms.

1. OHP
2. U shaped Seating arrangement
3. Round tables with chairs
4. Water
5. Writing Material
6. Notepads
7. Reading material
8. Laptop
9. LCD Screen
10. Blank Walls

Brain Dynamics

Now, if we don't use triggers, the training room that we design would be on the same lines as the DMP mapped above with minor modifications.

What is this 'DMP'?

DMP is the proverbial box when we use the verbiage 'out-of-the-box' thinking. In order to break out of the DMP, we have to use triggers. *Triggers are words which act as catalysts to access databases in the brain which were heretofore inaccessible.*

Triggers

Reality Modelling, Competency, Learning models, Enlightenment and Natural Colours

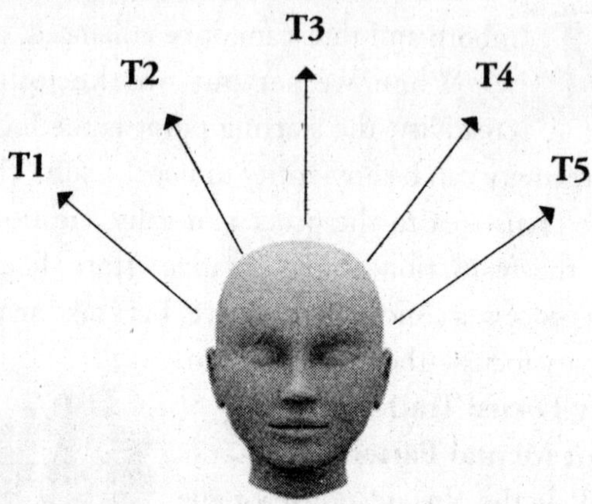

Every trigger yields ideas. A trigger enables the brain to access a mental database which was heretofore not in conscious access of

the brain. Every new mental database accessed by the brain when it is searching for a solurion yields new perspectives and approaches.

Once we have enriched our conscious database by using triggers,we can choose on the basis of cost-benefit analysis and the compulsions of practicality as to which of the ideas generated would form the final solution.

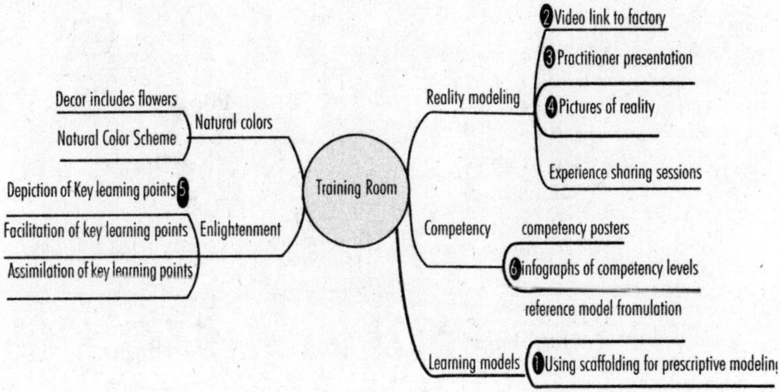

The solution for implementation can also be termed as the innovation dimensions, if the concept generated is new.

Training Room: Innovation Dimensions

1. Prescriptive modelling using scaffolding technique
2. Video link to factory
3. Practitioner presentations
4. Reality pictures
5. Depiction of key learning points

Process of new concept formation by utilising the Trigger scan

The identification of new triggers and their utilisation to form the trigger scan is crucial to the process of new concept formation. In case new triggers are not identified and utilised, we are not able to create new concepts. In fact, the concepts that we create would be incremental extensions of the concepts that already exist and predominate. In order to break into new mental pattern formation, the utilisation of new triggers is crucial. Otherwise, the level of newness in the generated concept would be zero.

Step 1: Formation of the Trigger Scan by utilising new triggers

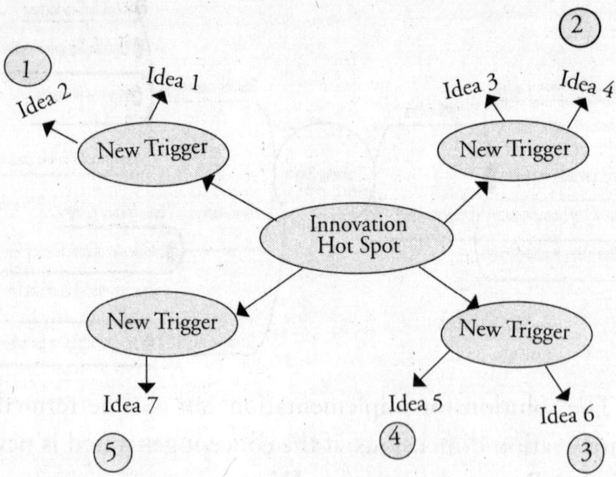

Step 2: Choosing and integrating new ideas into a new concept.

New Concepts

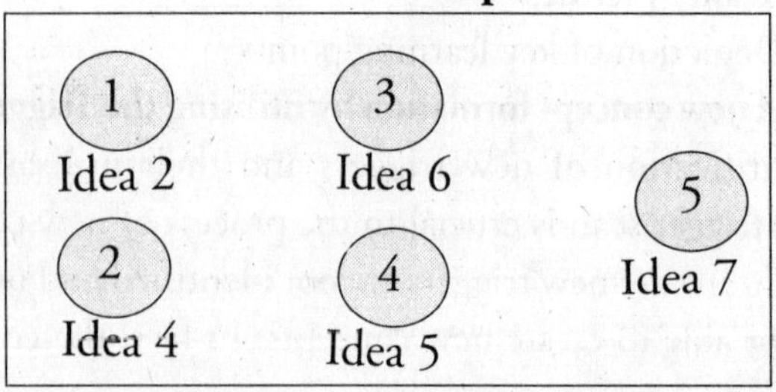

Quality of creativity

The quality of creativity is determined by the range of triggers used. There is direct correlation between the number of new triggers utilised and the newness of the solution generated. If the solution generated does not have the characteristic of newness then we have not generated an innovation. We need to go back to the creative thinking board and utilise a new range of triggers.

Creativity demands flexibility

The new concept created would not be a perfect fit to the context and limitations at hand. Therefore the new concept has to be adapted to the context parameters. If the original concept does not fit into our budget or is not aligned to contextual limitations then a transformation of it, an attribute of it or even element of it would fit into our budget.

Even if we implement an element of the new concept, we move out of the

'**Repetitive zone**' into the '**Creative zone**'.The trigger scan comes in handy for identifying and consolidating the ideas generated by using triggers.

This creative process is irreversible. **The new mental pattern triggered**, integrates into the original thought patterns, thereby changing the original mental pattern forever.

This creativity tool is called the TRIGGER SCAN. Although it resembles the mind map, it has significant points of difference. The key difference being the concept and utilisation of triggers as idea generators. Additionally the concept of quality of creativity emerges from the trigger scan. The range of new triggers used determines the quality of creativity. This determination was heretofore not possible in the technique of mind mapping.

Trigger Scan—Application Cases

Case: Flashlight powered by body heat

A 15-year-old girl in Canada has invented a flashlight that only needs the warmth of the hand to switch it on. Ann Makosinski, a high school junior in Victoria, British Columbia, was trying to think of a way of harvesting untapped energy when she was inspired to make the flashlight. She realised that the heat given out by the human body was an overlooked source of energy.

Her project objective was to create a flashlight that ran solely off the heat of the hand. That objective was accomplished when she discovered Peltier tiles, which produce electricity when one side of the tile is heated and the other is cooled.

Makosinski realised she could use these tiles to create energy for her flashlight if she left the device hollow.

Holding the flashlight on the outside would cause the tiles to heat up on one side while the ambient air would cool down the tile on the inside of the flashlight. The power created by the tiles was enough to power an LED light, but it did not create enough voltage. To troubleshoot that issue she created a circuit that would allow for transformers, upping the voltage, and it worked! The flashlight does have one issue: it works better in colder temperatures since the inside is able to cool down better in comparison to the person's body heat.

Case: Human bridge by the Indian Army

This creative solution to a problem is an example of Creative Problem Solving. Key Learning Point: New triggers are required for generating creative solutions .

Case: Toothpaste tube innovation

Focus: The focus is to design a new dispensation system which eliminates the need to squeeze tubes.

Brainwave Scan

Brainwave: The utilization of a lever to dispense toothpaste

New Value Created

1. No need of manually squeezing the tube.
2. No wastage of the left over paste.
3. Fixed consumption of paste.
4. Determination of number of usages left.

Triggering and Brainwaves

A lot of innovations have come about due to 'Brainwaves'. Since brainwaves come once in a blue moon, 'can we hang around waiting for one?'

If we examine the behavioural pattern of those personnel who have gotten a brainwave, we realise that they have an intense involvement in the subject. They have pursued the problem from multiple angles and have not found the solution. Subsequently, when they are in a state of relaxation the brainwave hits.

This indicates a correlation between triggering and brainwaves. When we use a trigger, it echoes in the brain. We do not know what database it will fuse with and thereby generate a potent innovation idea. However, we can increase the possibility of generating a potent innovation idea by increasing the number of triggers employed.

These triggers; their permutations and combinations; their cascading impact and their fusion with existing databases is what creates a brainwave.

Brainwave creation

Can there be a process for creating brainwaves?

If we had such a process, we would be able to create brainwaves at will. We would not be stuck in unending systems of stagnancy. We would not have to live with problems which have a tendency to sit on our heads while we stand helplessly watching them bury our vision and life under a rubble of impossibility.

Dynamics underneath brain wave creation

The dynamics underneath brain wave creation consist of utilising a wide range of triggers and an in depth utilisation of each trigger. Each trigger is connected to a mental database. The utilisation of each trigger results in the data coming out of the subconscious or the unconscious brain into the conscious brain and thus becoming available for a generation of creative solutions. The larger the range of triggers utilised, the greater is the probability of a brainwave.

Applying trigger scanning

Trigger scanning is a flexible and versatile creativity tool which can be utilised in almost all thinking situations in which we have to find new solutions. In fact, due to its simplicity of application, this should be the first creativity tool which an innovator needs to use. The utilisation of old and new triggers creates balance between continuity and creativity which is critical for the success of an innovation. The only weakness of the creativity tool is its inability to generate triggers for the innovator. The next tool of creativity, i.e. DMP challenge, does not have this limitation.

Where to apply trigger scanning?

Which is the road of least resistance and maximum impact for application of trigger scanning for generating innovations? The road starts from the Innovation Hotspots called, 'Problems'. Working back from the problems and utilising trigger scanning for designing the elements of the solution leads us to innovations.

Δ N Tool 2

DMP Challenge

Dominant Mental Pattern Challenge

The creativity tool DMP challenge enables the innovator to see his mental patterns and the change in mental patterns. It converts the art of creativity into a skill of creativity with the potential of endless repetition of a high level of creative thinking.

In order to decipher the phenomenon of DMP, we need to re-look at the learning process of the brain.

How does the brain learn when it receives a stimulus from the external environment?

When the brain receives a stimulus from the external environment, it forms a mental pattern through the interconnection of the neurons. The pattern formed by these neurons is called a mental pattern. When the same mental pattern gets repeated due to repetitive experience, the mental pattern becomes very strong and thick resulting in its becoming a preferred mental database to be accessed by the brain. This mental pattern is called the 'Dominant Mental Pattern'.

This dominant mental pattern is nothing but the proverbial

box when we talk about out-of-the box thinking.

Dominant Mental Pattern

The term 'DMP' (Dominant Mental Pattern) is one of the cornerstones of the Creativity & Innovation Process.

What is DMP?

It is the first response of the brain to a stimulus.

For example, when we say chair, we get a mental picture of an object with four legs, a back and a seat. This first response is the 'DMP of a Chair'.

We have DMPs with respect to every process, product or entity. The mapping of the DMP of a product indicates the end point of the existing mental pattern and the starting point of the new mental pattern.

Where the DMP ends, the zone of innovation starts.

The redesigning of this DMP is 'creativity' and it results in 'newness'. Newness is the starting point of the innovation development process. If there is no 'Newness', the resultant entity will never be categorised as an innovation.

Example: Innovation with respect to billboards that carry 'brands' of companies in the market place.

Purpose: Creation of market presence.

The DMP of a brand billboard is mapped below:

- Square or rectangular
- Colourful
- Lighted
- Brand name written in big letters
- Attached to a retailer shop
- Static

These are the elements of the Dominant Mental Pattern.

In order to innovate, this DMP has to be challenged.

On challenging the elements 'Brand names written in big Letters' and 'Static', we get the Trigger 'Why not dynamic?'. On developing this thought pattern, we get creative thought patterns such as:

- Brand billboard with a time clock.
- Brand billboard with a local population counter.
- Brand billboard with a pollution indicator

On challenging the shape, numerous creative ideas tend to emerge.

Through innovation a small company can take on a big company and win. That's how 'Apple' took on 'IBM' and won a big share in the PC Market.

We have heard the story of David versus Goliath. Let's revisit it from the angle of innovation. Two armies were going to war. The learned kings deliberated that the war outcomes would be decided on the basis of a fight between 2 warriors of the respective armies. One army fielded Goliath. He was 8ft tall and very strong. Nobody in the army came forward to face the might of Goliath. Finally David, a boy, volunteered. David refused to wear the armour offered to him. He used a slingshot to hit Goliath on the head with a stone, and knocked him unconscious.

If David had tried to beat 'Goliath on the basis of strength or armour, he would not have survived. He however won, because he changed the rules of the game.

This story reiterates the principle that through 'innovation' a small company can take on a big company and win.

Process of Utilising DMP Challenge

Step 1: Map the DMP of the in-focus product/process. When you hear the name of the product/process, an image forms in your mind. Note down what you see. This is the Dominant Mental Pattern. When you have made a comprehensive list of the DMP elements, what do you see in front of you?

You see a clear mirror image of the mental pattern in your mind with respect to the in-focus product/process.

This is the starting point of the Innovation process

Application Case 1: Chair

Dominant Mental Pattern of a Chair

- 4 legs
- Back
- Cushion
- Arms
- Plastic
- Wood
- For sitting
- Square

Step 2: Challenge the elements of the DMP by asking questions such as, 'What if this element is not there'?

Step 3: Utilize the sub-tool, "FRAME" to challenge the elements of the DMP.

F: Fuse two or more elements together

R:Replace an element with a new element

A:Add a new element to the set of elements

M:Magnify/Minify or mutate an element

E: Eliminate an element

Example: Replace the element, 'Cushion' with,'Fluid'.

Is the idea new?

Does Δ N exist?

If yes,we go on to the next step.

Step 4: Extract the value from the New Perspectives generated.

Example: A fluid filled seat would be more comfortable as compared to a cushioned seat.

Has new value been created?

Does Δ V exist?

If yes,we go on to the next step.

Step 5: Integrate the value extracted into the DMP for generating the new design.

Is there newness in design?

Does Δ D exist?

If yes,we prototype and test thereby generating an innovation

Application Case 2: Chocolate

Objective: To generate Product Innovations

Process:

Step 1: Map the DMP of chocolate

DMP (Chocolate)

Brown
Cuboid
Sweet
Rectangular
Nuts
Calories
Children
Gold and Silver Wrapper

Step 2: Challenge the DMP of chocolate

1. Challenge the first element of the DMP: Brown
   - What if it is not brown; it is green, yellow, blue or red?
2. Challenge the second element of the DMP: Cuboidal
   - What if it is not cuboidal; it is conical, cylindrical or spherical?
3. Challenge the third element of the DMP: Sweet
   - What if it is not sweet; it is sour, chilly, salty and tangy?
4. Challenge the fourth element of the DMP: Rectangular
   - What if it is not rectangular; it is oval or it is in the shape of Superman, batman, cartoon characters or Pokemon characters? What if it is in the shape of a country's map, heart or is shaped like a doll?
5. Challenge ingredients: Nuts
   - What if there are no nuts; there is cheese or liquor?

All these challenges yield new product concepts. One or more of these concepts can be combined together to increase the potency of the new product concept. Needless to say, all product concepts do not have value as innovations. Value descends into these product concepts, if they satisfy some unique requirement of the consumer or a stakeholder.

Step 3: Use FRAME. The abbreviation FRAME can be utilised to generate triggers. This is the advantage that DMP challenge has over the TRIGGER SCAN. DMP challenge provides the triggers which can be utilised to break into the creative space. Let's use 'Replace' from FRAME.

FRAME
F=Fuse
R=Replace
A=Add
M=Mutate,Magnify,
Minify
E=Eliminate

3.1 Replacing 'gold and silver wrapper' (element of the DMP) with an educational game for children. The cost of the wrapper with the educational game would only be incrementally different from that of the gold and silver wrapper, but it would satisfy another need of the consumer. Thus, the range of needs satisfied by the product would be more without any additional costs incurred. The result is increased value to the user.

Step 4: Use FADE

FADE
F=fuse
A=Alternative
D=DMP
E=Elements

4.1 For each of the elements of the DMP, we generate alternatives.

DMP Alternatives
Color: Red
Shape: Conical

Taste: Tangy
Value: High sentimental value
4.2 We fuse the alternatives together to generate the 'New Product' concept.
4.3 We connect the 'New Product concept' to 'Needs' of the consumer and see if some unique need is satisfied. If yes, and if we are able to lay down the specifications of the product Innovation, *we have a potent innovation idea.*
This has to be prototyped and tested, before it can be rolled out as an innovation.

Where the DMP ends, there is a slight vacuum. This vacuum precedes the formation of new mental patterns.

Application Case 3: Media Innovations

This is a niche application of DMP challenge.Creativity is considered to be crucial in the advertising industry. When we see an advertisement on TV or in the print media, we comment on the creativity involved. This is one kind of creativity in the advertisement world. The second kind of creativity is in terms of developing media innovations to act as a vehicle for the tagline of a product.

A niche application of, 'DMP challenge' is in this process of generating media innovations.

The process of its utilisation for generating media innovations for a garment manufacturer, 'Zy' with the tagline, 'Brilliant colours of Zy' is given below:
Step 1: Mapping of the dominant mental pattern associated with the tagline, 'Brilliant colours of Zy'.

DMP of Tag line, 'Brilliant colors of ZY'

- Clothes
- Colour
- Right
- Ethical
- Good for humanity
- Unity
- People
- Shirts
- Paints

Step 2: The innovator utilises every element of the DMP as a trigger:

Trigger 1: Color

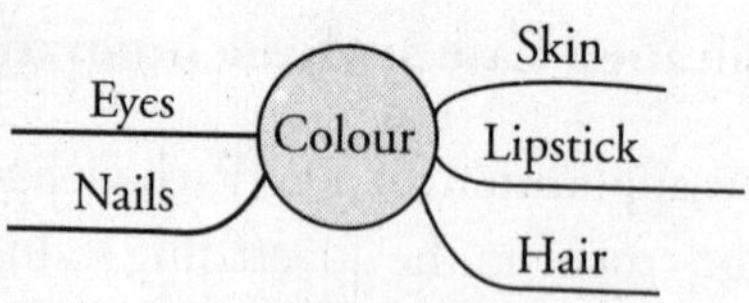

Resultant Brainwaves:Depiction of different coloured eyes along with the tagline, "Brilliant colours of Zy".

- Depiction of different colours of lips along with the tagline, 'Different colours of Zy'.
- Depiction of different colours of hair along with the tagline

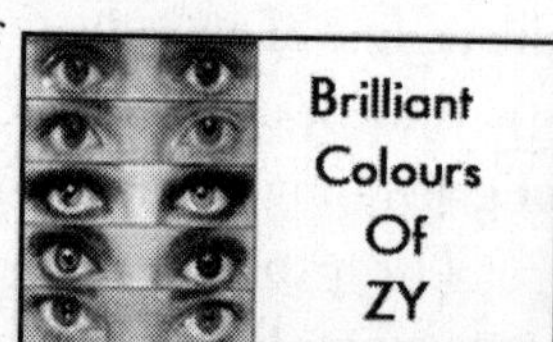

Thus the process of new mental pattern formation (Δ N) involving DMP challenge is mapped below:

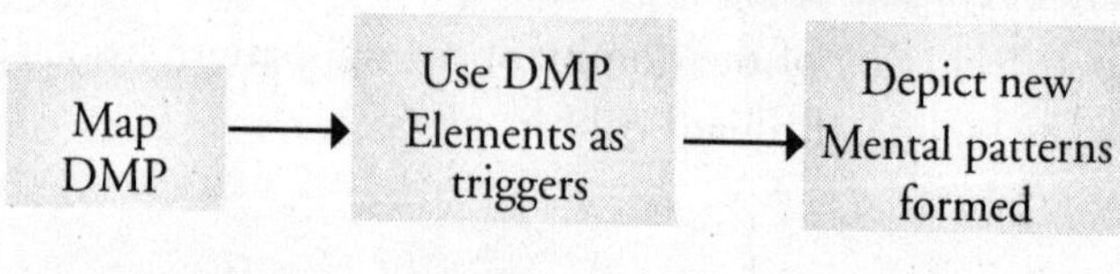

Thus, DMP challenge can be a source of unlimited newness in any concept or entity.

Application Case 4: Product Innovation (Mosquito Repellent)

Step 1: DMP Mapping of mosquito repellent

DMP Element	Function	Value
Mosquito repellent fluid (DEET)	• Repel mosquitoes • Moisturise skin	• Protection from mosquito bites • Better skin
Plastic bottle	• Storage of DEET	• Usable over a period of time
Electrode	• Capillary action	• Suction of DEET
Electricity Device	• Usage of electric current in coil for evaporation of DEET	• Evaporation of DEET

In this DMP we have included two additional aspects of the DMP i.e. **function and value**. These two elements add substance to the DMP and make it more comprehensive. It also clearly specifies the needs being satisfied in terms of the value being created.

Now the challenge is to create new value by challenging the elements of the DMP and, thereby, mutating the functions.

Step 2: Challenging DEET

Step 3: Identifying the new value created by the alternatives and integrating the alternative that creates the maximum value

DMP Alternatives (Δ N)	Function	Value (Δ V)
Citronella	Natural mosquito repellent	Effective
Lavender oil	• Repels mosquitoes • Scent	• Moderately effective • Pleasant ambience

Step 4: Integrating the new elements for creating the Innovative solution

DMP Element	Function	Value
Citronella oil	• Repels mosquitoes	• Protection from mosquito bites
Lemongrass oil	• Repels mosquitoes • Aroma therapy • Reduces anxiety	• Protection from mosquito bites • Aromatic • Clean and calming ambience
Plastic bottle	• Storage of oil	• Usable over a period of time

Electrode	• Capillary action	• Suction of oil
Electricity Device	• Usage of electric current in coil for evaporation of oil	• Evaporation of oil

These new set of DMP elements constitute the design of the innovation.

Core and peripheral elements of the DMP

All the elements of the DMP are not equally important in terms of the value that they create for the user.The elements of the DMP that create the fundamental or the core value to the user are the core elements of the DMP and the one's that create perepheral value to the user are called the peripheral elements of the DMP.

Hence ,DEET' in the aforementioned case is the core element of the ,"Mosquito repellent" while the others are the peripheral elements.

Thus,on challenging a core element of the DMP,the resultant innovation is more valuable in comparison to a challenge of a peripheral element of the DMP.

Case

Vertical Substation by Reliance Infrastructure in Mumbai.

The conventional AIS substation is horizontal. The design is reminiscent of a bygone era when there was plentiful supply of land. However, in the current scenario, since there is an acute shortage of land, the earlier solution doesn't work.

The innovative solution to this problem was found by Reliance Infrastructure, who created a vertical substation. The space required by the vertical GIS substation is 3500sm while the conventional AIS substation requires 40,000 square meters of space .

This is an example of the application of, 'DMP Challenge' for finding innovative solutions in areas where the current solution has become saturated.

Then, the question arises." Where to apply DMP Challenge"?

DMP challenge is to be applied where:

- The existing solution has saturated. It won't improve any more.
- There is a need for quantum innovation rather than incremental innovation.

Δ N
Tool 3

Multi-Fusion

Multi-fusion

When we fuse two different domains together a new domain gets created.

Internet= Domain 1

Commerce=Domain 2

Internet + Commerce=E-Commerce

If we consider the mental pattern of a product or process and cross fertilise it with a totally different mental pattern, a new mental pattern gets formed. On closely examining the products around us, the utilisation of cross-fertilisation becomes apparent.

Ex: Paddle + boat = Paddleboat

Cushion + boat = Hovercraft

Human beings are also created as a result of the cross-fertilisation of a male and a female. Thus, it comes to the fore that nature uses cross-fertilisation as a basic tool for creativity and regeneration whether it is in plants or animals.

If the tool is so powerful why not use it in other areas?

Example: Poetry through fusion and metaphor.

How does a poet manage to create powerful imagery? What makes a poet's writing interesting? Why do we get a feeling of 'pleasure' and 'insight' when we read a good poem?

One of the tools that a poet utilises is a 'Metaphor'. The utility of this tool is visible in this poem titled 'Her'.

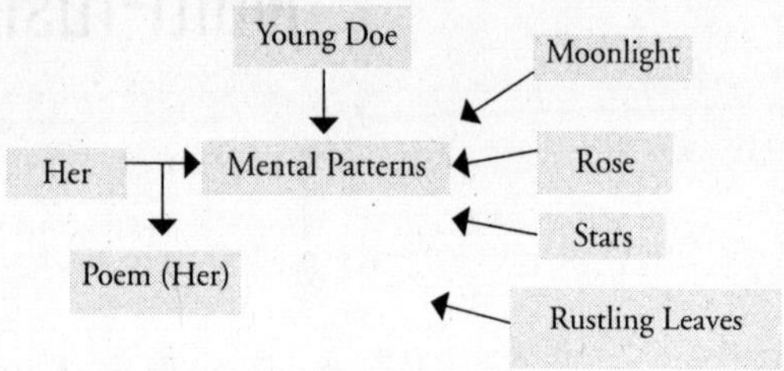

Her

Her lips are petals of a red rose,
Her face the colour of moonlight,
Her eyes are shimmering stars on a dark night,
Her voice echoes the sound of rustling leaves,
and her walk is of a young doe.

What is the underlying principle?

The poet takes the mental pattern related to 'Her' and fuses it with a diverse range of powerful mental patterns related to a rose, moonlight, dark night, rustling leaves and a young doe. **The result of this multi fusion is a poem.**

Multi fusion can be a source of infinite innovations. The process of utilising this tool is mapped below:

Step 1: Map the Dominant Mental Pattern of the product/process.

Step 2: Identify Fusion objects. Fuse these DMP objects into the DMP of the in-focus product/process. If the fusion creates additional value in terms of satisfaction of additional needs of the user, select the idea for prototyping. Otherwise let it go and move on to the next fusion.

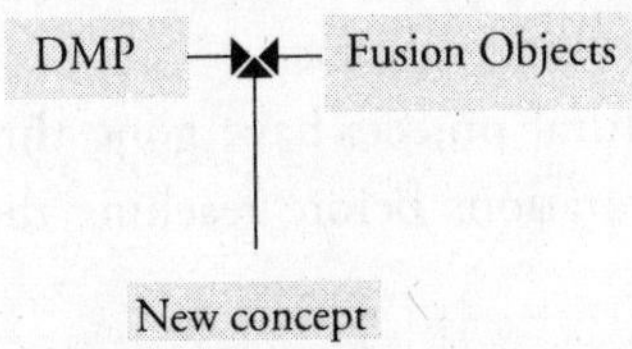

Step 3: Identify objects which are outside the Dominant Mental Pattern with respect to the in-focus product/process. Try to fuse these into the DMP of the product/process. If the fusion creates value, select the idea for prototyping, otherwise move on to the next fusion.

Step 4: Identify 'Objects from Nature' such as a flower, a waterfall, a drop of water, a watermelon etc. Fuse the object into the DMP of the in-focus product/process. In case new value gets created, select the idea for prototyping. Otherwise, move on to the next fusion.

In order to identify the objects from nature, the innovator must try to answer the question, "how does nature solve the same problem?"

In case no natural objects are identified as a result of this trigger, the innovator needs to pick up generic natural objects.

Multi fusion can be a source of an inexhaustible supply of 'innovations'. However, in order to benefit from it, the innovator needs to apply the tool with due diligence and at the same time practice flexibility. S/he needs to develop the skill of letting go of ideas that add no value.

Thus, a quick formation of new mental patterns and their quick rejection if there is no new value created forms the core of the Innovation process.

The sub tool of 'Fusion with nature' is extremely powerful and can be treated as an independent tool of Innovation. Natural objects display an element of excellence that is rarely present in man-made objects.

These natural objects have gone through innumerable number of mutations before reaching their current level of excellence.

It would be impossible to manufacture an orange, should we try it. Building even a shade of this excellence into our products would result in innovation.

This reinforces the fact that creativity as a skill can be consciously developed. It also shows that creative output is a result of focused effort and needs a lot of discipline.

It has been felt that creativity and discipline are opposites and that the practice of discipline hinders creativity.

Fusion Objects	
Parameter benchmarks	IT
Nature	Out-of-DMP objects

The fact is that 'discipline' is an essential ingredient in the formation of creative output. Without discipline of focus and skill application, creativity does not occur.

This is the dynamic that underlies creativity through fusion. There are multiple systems of fusion that enable us to create new concepts and unleash our imagination. These multiple systems have been integrated into a tool titled 'Multi-fusion'. Whenever this dynamic is triggered it creates new entities. However, the failure rate of these creations is high. On the basis of the success and failure pattern of innovations, it has been realised that certain kinds of fusion have a greater probability of creating a successful innovation. These kinds of fusions have morphed into the innovation tool 'Multi-fusion'.

Fundamental principle

The fundamental principle underneath this power tool is that when one fuses two different mental patterns, a new mental pattern gets created. Creative dynamics are unleashed by fusion of different domains.

Example: Sanskrit was a language spoken in ancient India. Tamil is spoken predominantly in Tamil Nadu (an Indian state). These different languages domains fused together historically to create a new language called 'Malayalam' which is spoken in Kerala, a state at the southern tip of India.

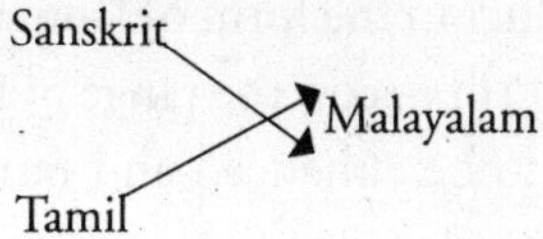

Another example is that of the MRI Scan (Magnetic Resonance Imaging). It is more effective in comparison to the CT (Computed Tomography) Scan for imaging the internal parts of the body. It is the output of the fusion of the two knowledge domains of nuclear science and anatomy. The MRI scan provides much better contrast between different soft tissues of the body as compared to the CT scan .

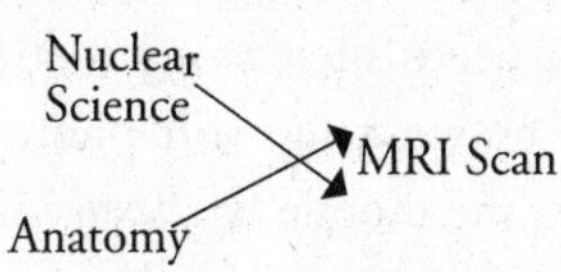

Fusion for innovation

The domains which can be a rich source of innovation through fusion are:

- Fusion of new functions
- Fusion with function benchmarks
- Fusion with IT
- Fusion with Nature

Fusion tool 1: Fusion of new functions

Fusion of new functions is the most prevalent form of innovation.

What does it mean?

It means, adding a new capability into the product. Underlying principle:A product or service exists because it satisfies a need. In order to satisfy an identified need, capability needs to be built into the product in the form of "function". If we want to satisfy a wider range of needs, the range of functions built into the product need to be enhanced and mutated. This process leads to innovation.

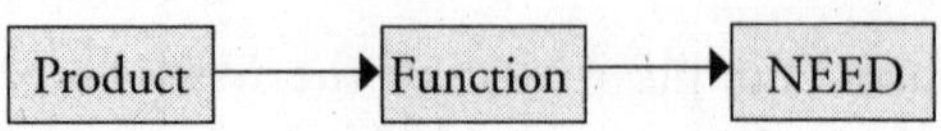

Case in point: Mobile Phone

The case in point which highlights this process is the evolution of the mobile. Initially it was designed to satisfy the need of voice communication. Subsequently, new functions were integrated into the product design in order to satisfy a wider range of consumer needs such as internet connectivity, word processing, social networking, still photography and video photography.Thus, the mobile has been innovating at a rapid pace by adding new functions into the product.

Product	Function	Need
Mobile	Mobile link over a cellular network of base stations	Voice interaction
Mobile+Computer	• Mobile link over cellular network • GPRS connectivity • Office Productivity tools • Video camera	• Voice interaction • Internet connectivity • Office document processing • Social networking • Videography.

Case in point: Orbit chewing gum

Orbit, the chewing gum has an enhanced set of functions. Traditionally the chewing gum contains flavour and sugar which makes it tasty. However, in the case of orbit new functions have been added to increase the range of needs satisfied. The new functions being removal of stains, teeth whitening and a clean feeling.The underlying principle of this innovation is the addition of new functions to the product in alignment with a wider range of consumer needs.

Case in point: A/c cum air cleaner

What is the main function of the A/c. It provides cool air for controlling the temperature of a room. It satisfies the human need of comfortable environmental temperature.

A new need of 'Clean air' is becoming more and more dominant with the increasing levels of pollution and the increasing incidence of lung diseases such as lung cancer and asthma. Hence, there is an innovation opportunity for integrating the function of 'cleaning of air' along with the existing cooling function of the a/c.

Such an innovation is bound to attract a hefty premium in terms of product price.

Case in point: Pen tablet

The pen tablet is going to make the mouse redundant because its range of functions far exceed those of the mouse. A mouse is used for dragging the cursor around the computer screen and for the inputting of commands through left or right clicks.

A pen tablet on the other hand not only does the functions of a mouse, it also enables hand made drawings on the computer screen, hand signatures and annotations on computer graphics. The result is enhanced value to the customer.

Value=(Benefits/Costs)

What is the impact on the product price? How much is the customer willing to pay for the satisfaction of a wider range of needs?

The answer to this question is evident from the price of the pen tablet which is approximately five times that of the mouse.

Case in point: Swiss army knife

The design integrates a range of functions that are in consonance with the range of needs.

Impact of fusion of new function:

The direct impact of the addition of new functions into the product depends on 'Benefits to the user'. However, the over-all value of the product to the customer would only increase if the increase in benefit is more than the increase in the price of the product. The success of the innovation is critically dependent on 'Product value'.

Product value = Benefits/Costs

Fusion tool 2 : Fusion with Function benchmarks

In order to innovate through 'Fusing with Function benchmarks', we need to answer the following series of questions:

Q. What are the components of the product?

Q. What are the functions being performed by each component?

Q. What is the benchmark for each function?

Q. What process does the benchmark use?

Can the process be integrated into our product or service?

If we can generate the answers to all the above questions, we have made significant progress on the path of innovation and we are close to our destination.

Case: Automobile air conditioners

Q. What is the function being performed?

A. Cooling effect to all passengers in the car.

Q. What is the benchmark for this function?

A. Air conditioners for home cooling.

Q. What processes does the benchmark use?

A. The processes being used:

- Swing function for stabilising and evening out climate control.
- Follow function for following the occupant in the room.

- Kiamin function for changing the temperature in consonance with body temperature.

Q. Can these processes be integrated into the car air conditioner?

A. Yes

So we need to learn the process from the benchmark function and integrate it into our product, thereby enabling it to innovate. The result would be car air conditioners with the swing function,the follow-me function and the kiamin function.

Case: Automobile headlights

Q. What is the function being performed?

A. Lighting up of a surface.

Q. What is the function benchmark for this function?

A. LCD projectors.

Q. What is the process adopted by the LCD projector?

A. Light reaches the target area and spreads.

Q. Can we integrate this process into automobile head lamps?

A. Yes.

The result would be automobile head lamps which are far more effective than the current headlamps in terms of balanced lighting of the road surface.

Case: Scratches on cars

Car paint has a tendency to get scratched during the production process. This results in high cost of rework.

Q. What is the function to be performed?

A. To stop the paint surface from getting scratched.
Q. What is the benchmark for this function?
A. In mobiles a thin plastic film is pasted onto the screen of the mobile, thereby protecting it from scratches.
Q. Can it be integrated with cars?
A. Yes.

Hence, this is a viable innovation which would reduce paint scratches thereby reducing the cost of rework.

Case: Screws in a car wheel

Q. What is the function to be performed?
A. Attach the wheel to the car.
Q. What is the benchmark for this function?
A. In formula 1 racing cars one screw is used to attach the wheel to the car.

Q. Why do we use 4 screws to attach the wheel to the car?
Why not three, two or even one? Have we explored?
A. No.
Q. Can a prototype be made and tested with 3 as well as 2 screws?
A. Yes.

There is a potential innovation , which would have a direct impact on inventory of screws, cost of the car and the ease of changing the tire in case of a puncture. This innovation is visible in TATA NANO, the cheapest car in the world being produced in India.

Case: Reducing wastage of power cables

The Problem:Power cables in power plants are issued in standard lengths say 100 meters. For a given task, varying length of the power cable is utilised say 10 meters or 24 meters. The remaining part of the power cable lies around and rots in the sun. The challenge: To eliminate power cable wastage when it is issued in standard lengths in power plants. Fusion Tool to be used: Function benchmarking

Q. What is the function requirement?

A. Varying length of the power cable as per the requirement.

Q. Where is this function performed without the accompanying wastage? (functional benchmarking)

A. Kite string storage and dispersal.

Q. How is the function performed?

A. The kite string is stored on a roller pin by a shopkeeper. The shopkeeper extracts the exact amount of kite string as per requirement of the customer and there is no resultant wastage.

Q. Can the same process be used for disbursing power cables?

A. yes.

This yields a new process for disbursing power cables. Power cables are stored on large roller pins. The exact amount of the cable required is extracted and cut. Thus, power cable wastage is eliminated.

Case: Fuel efficiency enhancement

The problem:The car a/c draws its power from the engine of the car thereby reducing its power and also reducing fuel efficiency by as as much as 40%. How can we use "Functional bench-marking" to resolve this problem?

The challenge:The car a/c should not draw power from the car engine. Fusion Tool to be used: Function bench-marking

Q. What is the function being performed?

A. The engine is supplying power to the car a/c.

Q. In which other industry is the same function performed?

A. Home inverter industry. The inverter supplies power to the electrical instruments at home.

Q. Can the same process be integrated into the automobile systems?

A. Yes

Car A/c → Inverter → Electrical socket

Functional Benchmark: Home inverter

The home inverter provides power to the entire home and it is charged through electricity. Can it be utilised to power the car a/c? If the answer to this question is "Yes" we have an innovation in our hands.

Design and utility

An inverter is integrated into the bonnet of the car. This inverter is used to power the car a/c. It is recharged through an electric socket. This reduces the pressure on the car engine, thereby enhancing fuel efficiency.

One key characteristic of the process of function bench-marking is that it is employed across industrial boundaries. One enables innovation by learning from other industries as to how they solve the same problem or they do the same function. The resultant innovation has a high probability of success since the process is already working in a different context. It requires customisation and mutation. It does not need to be designed from scratch.

Innovation Levers

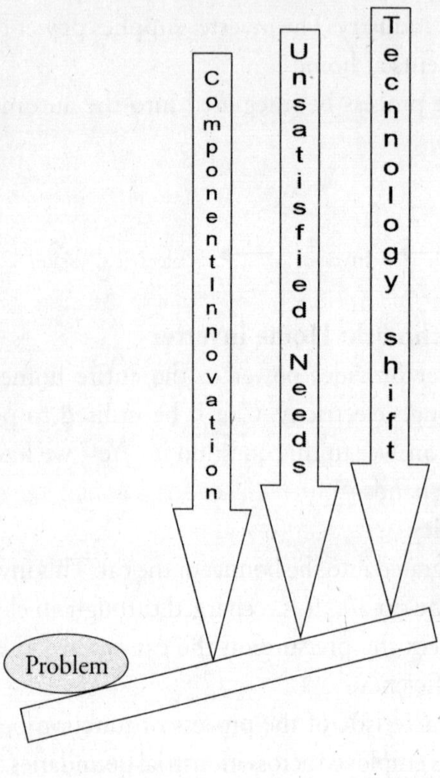

Innovation Levers

All the innovation tools that we have examined till now enable the innovator to design the innovation idea from scratch. This approach is powerful because it enables the innovator to break into the creative zone.

However there also exist innovation levers which enable the innovator to build on already existing entities in order to innovate.

Leveraging component Innovation

This lever of innovation is frequently used by computer hardware manufacturers for up grading their products by integrating new versions of micro-processors or software. However, the underlying lever of innovation is not crystallised in order to enable its application to all work domains.

As we dig deeper into underlying patterns, we can see a similarity between this lever and systemic innovation. Underlying principle of Leveraging component innovation, 'A product consists of multiple components. Each of the components is a part of a different industry. Each component is innovating at a different frequency. This innovation dynamic can be utilised to leverage component innovation for continuous product innovation. On replacing the existing component with the innovated component, the interaction of the component with the other product components enhances the product's efficacy. Thus, our product innovates without having to innovate from scratch.'

Case: Social Media

A law firm adopted the social media approach to marketing its services. Thus it developed a blog called 'Timesoflaw. blogspot.com'. It also developed accounts on twitter, google + and linkedIn.

The marketing strategy was effective. However, it was extremely cumbersome. Then along came a component innovation called HOOTSUITE. This blog innovation enabled the updating of multiple blogs by making one post in Hootsuite. The adoption of Hootsuite, thus, enabled innovation in the social media marketing process of the law firm.

The only problem with this innovation lever is that the possibilities it throws up are faster than our ability to convert them into reality. Our conceptual limitations can slow us down in the process of leveraging component innovations.

Case: Customer relationship management for INSYCON.

Customer relationship management was a big problem for this management consultancy firm. Customer related data was manually recorded and utilised by its management consultants. The organisation tried to innovate on this by developing a relational database of customers which was connected to the computers of all the management consultants such that if one consultant added a new customer, the central database would update. Though this process innovation was powerful, it failed to become the norm because of it being cumbersome. Then a component innovation that occurred was a open source mobile application. This enabled the maintenance of customer related data on the mobile of each consultant and thus was instrumental in the enhancement of the efficacy of the CRM system in the organisation.

The challenge is to 'Leverage component innovation' continuously rather than once in a while. Most of the time these innovation opportunities go a-begging because of inadequate attention to this innovation lever.

Leveraging Unsatisfied Needs

A product or a process exists because it satisfies some needs of a consumer. User needs are the single most success determining factor of a product/service.

Let's examine this pattern through examination of a product 'natural flowers'.

Case: Natural Flowers

Needs satisfied	Needs unsatisfied
-Gifting	-Longevity
-Conveys feelings	-Disintegrates
-Fragrance	
-Freshness	
-Colourful	
-Pleasing to the senses	

Customer Needs analysis

Unsatisfied needs as triggers of innovation The un-satisfied needs act as triggers of innovation. Working back from the unsatisfied needs if we do reverse engineering, we can arrive at product innovations with a low risk of failure. Unsatisfied needs translate into the creation of new value, ie. Δ V.

In order to fulfil the unsatisfied needs related to longevity, if an organisation manufactures flowers which last 10 days rather than 2 days when set in salty water, it would result in an innovation which can command a higher market price and enhanced sales resulting in increased market share.

Satisfied Needs as triggers of innovation: Fragrance is one of the needs satisfied by the current product—a fresh cut flower. If we create flowers which have higher fragrance as compared to current flowers, the product would differentiate itself in the market and could be higher priced. This could be achieved either through bio genetics or by simply spraying the flowers with their own concentrated fragrance.

Building on the Dominant need of 'Conveying Feelings', a sales process innovation emerges in the form of a 'Feelings Inventory' and the corresponding 'Flower combinations'. This feeling - flower combination could be given to every retailer. This would enable the customer to create bouquets customised to his/her feelings.

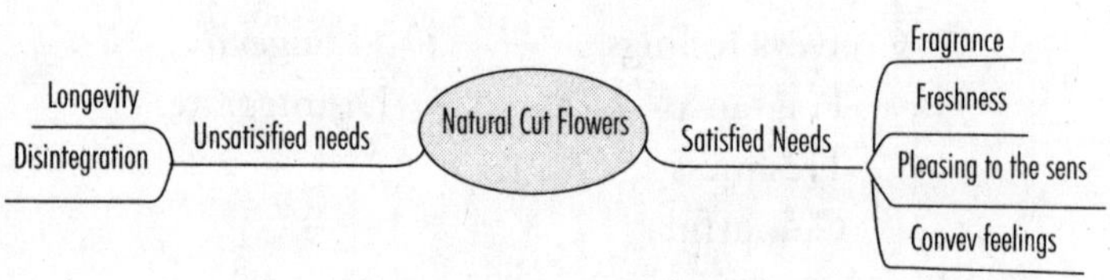

Product innovations

- Classification of flowers on the basis of longevity.
- Natural flower dowsed in its own concentrated fragrance.
- Feelings inventory based bouquets.

New Needs and Need Clusters

There is a widespread notion that there are limited unknown needs and that needs are already known and a given which is not true. Needs are in a continuous state of flux. The satisfaction of current 'Dominant Needs' gives rise to new needs. Let us illustrate this phenomenon through an example.

For example, if you do not own a home computer, and there is a major demand from your spouse and child for one. Your child wants to play computer games while your spouse wants to use it as an educational tool.

As soon as you buy the home computer and these needs are satisfied; a new need arises, that is 'to play live and interactive games on the net with children in other countries'. The new need that arises is that of 'Video Conferencing'.

In order to satisfy these NEW needs, you need to subscribe to an Internet connection; buy a Digital Video Camera and related software.

This example illustrates that 'New Needs' keep on arising all the time and that these new needs are 'Innovation Triggers'. A joker in this pack of needs is the existence of 'Latent Needs'.

Latent Needs: These are needs which do not exist within the perception of either the customer or the industry. It is only when the product or service is produced that the Latent need surfaces and becomes dominant. The product 'Walkman' of 'Sony' is a typical case-in-point.

Need Dynamics As one set of needs get satisfied, new needs arise to take their place and latent needs come to the surface. As we design innovations, to satisfy the new needs, heretofore unknown and latent needs arise to the surface and become dominant.

Thus, we move from innovation to innovation and the need for innovation remains a continuous phenomenon.

Innovations may come and innovations may go but the need for innovation goes on forever.

Unsatisfied needs or the better satisfaction of currently satisfied needs act as triggers of product or process Innovations.

Potent Innovations result, if we work backwards from these needs and redesign the product. This however, does not mean that unsatisfied/latent /current needs are the only and sole triggers of innovations.

This is one of the patterns that lead to innovation. The second pattern starts from product design. Challenging the Dominant Mental Pattern of the product may result in a product design where it can connect to latent customer needs resulting in breakthrough Innovation.

This dynamic character of needs gives rise to the phenomenon of 'Innovation clusters'.

The phenomenon of Innovation Clusters When the current set of needs are satisfied, new needs arise and become dominant. Hence 'needs move in clusters' and since needs move in clusters, innovations also move in clusters.

Therefore, if we want to increase the "level of Innovation" in an organisation, start by getting at least one innovation accepted. This Innovation will unleash a dynamic generation of new needs, thereby catalysing a cluster of innovations around it, over a period of time.

An alternative application of this learning is that organisations can predict as to which new needs would arise when the current needs get satisfied.

Working back from the expected new needs, organisations can design and store prototypes to be unleashed as soon as the new needs start becoming dominant.

The disciplined practice of this process would enable an organisation to don the mantle of leadership in 'Innovation'.

Leveraging technology shifts

When we talk about technology shifts, some fundamental questions arise.

What is a technology shift?

What triggers a technology shift?

What is the impact of a technology shift?

How do we leverage technology shifts?

In order to understand technology shifts, we need to first understand the life curve of a technology which is called the 'Technology Curve'. A technology curve is also the visual representation of a technology. Without this representation, technology is a nebulous concept.

The technology curve on the parameters of value created by the technology on the Y-axis and time on the X-axis is in the shape of an elongated S.

The technological life cycle has three distinct stages:

Birth stage (Stage 1)

Technology is born; prototypes are made; prototype failures are routine. The value generated by the innovation is negative.

Growth stage (Stage 2) The technology has solved its teething problems and overcome the critical glitches to its functioning. The range of needs satisfied increase thereby, enhancing the value created by the innovation. The economies of scale reduce the costs. Hence, the new technology grows rapidly due to widespread acceptance.

Saturation and decline (Stage 3) The technology has reached its natural limits of value creation. The technology has reached its saturation level. Even if improvement happens after reaching this level, the increase in value will be negative because the costs will exceed the new benefits created by the improvement in technology.

Technology shift

A technology shift happens when a completely new technological approach creates substantially more value in comparison to the existing one.

What triggers a technology shift?

When a new technology creates more value than the existing technology for all its stakeholders, the juggernaut of a technology shift gets catalysed.

Case-in-point:

Technology shift from Incandescent bulb to CFL to LED bulb. The dynamics unleashed by a technology shift are such that we can only ignore them to our peril. A technology shift is either an opportunity or a threat. If we leverage the technology shift for generating innovation, it is an opportunity, otherwise it is a threat.

Leveraging technology shifts: The systems at our work or home consist of multiple elements. Leveraging the technology shift in any of these elements enables us to remain at the cutting edge of efficacy.

Case: RFID
(Radio Frequency Identification)

RFID: A Technology shift

RFID is a technology shift in the area of identification and tracking of objects. This has numerous applications in the areas of inventory management and process innovation.

This is a technology shift from barcoding. Barcoding requires data input by a human whereas RFID does not require human interface.

How does RFID work ?

A RFID Tag is connected to every object. The RFID Tag consists of an antenna and a chip for storing information regarding the object. RFID towers are erected after every 100 meters. The object is tracked through radio wave interaction between the tower and the RFID tag.

Leveraging RFID as a technology shift Applications:

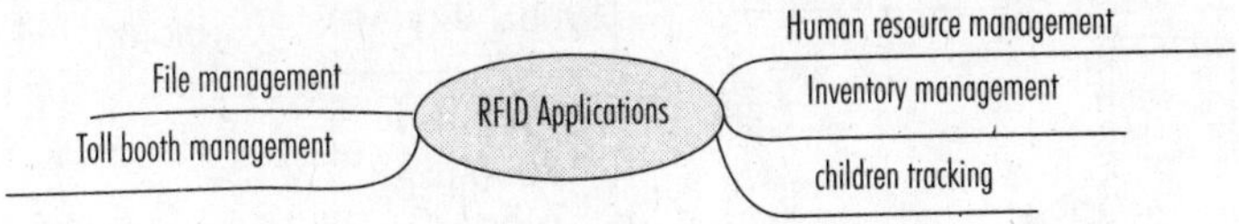

Value Analysis regarding acquisition of a technology shift

Leveraging technology shifts is a powerful system of functioning at the cutting edge. However, the decision as to when to acquire the technology shift is critical to the success of the resultant process innovation. If acquired too early the glitches would be many, thereby destroying rather than creating new value. If acquired too late, the lead position would be handed over to the institution that acquires it first.

Thus what is the right time to acquire a technology shift?

The right time to acquire a technology shift is when the technology is moving from its birth stage to the high growth stage. Objecting to a technology shift because one's business is related to the older technology is a sure shot method of failure. However, a lot of successful organisations have made this fatal mistake time and again. Not leveraging a technology shift or even leveraging it too late lead to stagnation and decline.

Case: Inkjet printers to laser printers

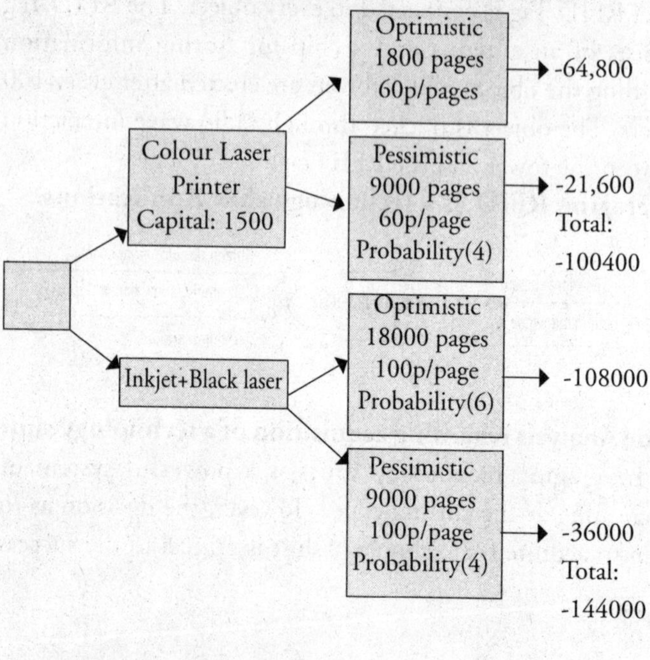

Decision trees can be very effectively utilised to calculate the value being created by technology shifts. A management consultancy was using inkjet printers in its offices. The inkjet printers were functioning fine. So there was no need to scan for the acquisition of new printers. Laser printers appeared in the market. These were a technology shift. However, they were expensive. With the rapid adoption of laser printers their prices began to fall. So, whether the technology shift should be acquired by the consultancy was a moot question. This question can be answered through value analysis. When the value created by the technology shift outstrips the value created by the current technology, it is time to leverage the technology shift.

In order to conduct a comparative value analysis of the two technologies, we divide the future into 2 scenarios namely, the optimistic scenario and the pessimistic scenario, and calculate the comparative cost of utilising the comparative technologies.

Value Analysis

The aforementioned value analysis indicates that the cost of the technology shift over a 5 year life period is less than the cost of operating the existing technology. Thus, the time is optimal for leveraging the technology shift.

We have not analysed the benefit aspect of the value analysis yet. If we take into consideration the additional benefits of utilising colour laser in terms of efficacy and comprehension, then the value differential of the technology shift vis-a-vis the existing technology would be even higher. Thus the impact of not leveraging a technology shift becomes obvious in terms of higher costs and loss of differential benefits of the new technology.

Patents as innovation barometers

N determines the level of newness in the new concept generated. It is the deciding parameter which will determine the categorisation of the new concept as innovative. It also is a critical parameter to determine whether the resultant innovation is patentable or not. If N=zero then the new concept is not patentable.

In order to develop an acceptable level of N, we use all the tools and levers heretofore enunciated in this book. However, a key question remains.

How do we determine whether N exists in a concept?

For that purpose we need to use a source of knowledge that is perhaps the most under-utilised knowledge source, i.e.patent databases. Patent databases are open databases. They can easily be accessed via the internet. They are an inexhaustible source of knowledge and triggers.

The related patents in these databases can be utilised to determine whether N exists in a concept. In case the concept already exists in these patent databases, then N=zero and we need to go back to the drawing board and generate more triggers in order to enhance N. If we do not utilise the patent databases as a reference point to determine N, our entire innovation effort may go in vain because what we end up prototyping after a lot of effort may already be patented and we may achieve nothing other than patent infringement.

Thus, the existing patents related to a concept are a critical reference point to determine N in the concept. However, the utility of accessing related patents does not end there. The patents can also be utilised as sources of triggers. Knowledge cannot be patented. Only forms of it in the forms of concepts can be patented. The inherent knowledge can be leveraged by anyone for R& D or to create something brand new. The key parameter is that N should exist in the new entity created.

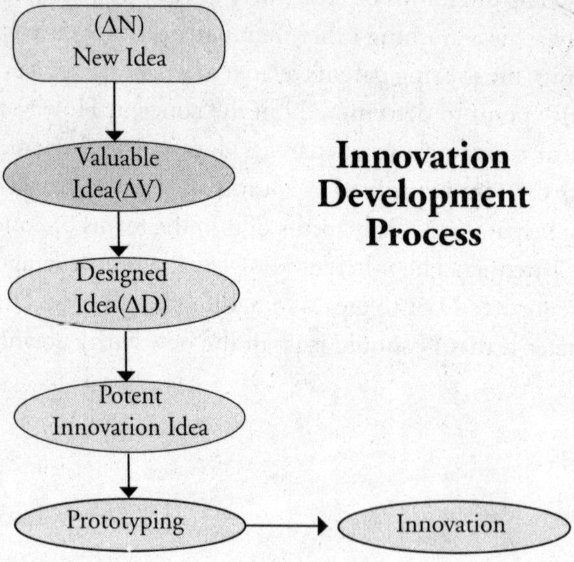
(ΔN)
New Idea
Valuable
Idea(ΔV)
Designed
Idea(ΔD)
Potent
Innovation Idea
Prototyping
Innovation
Innovation
Development
Process

Idea Value

Every new idea is not a valuable idea. Only valuable ideas can be taken forward to the design stage. Every subsequent stage in the innovation development process takes a lot of effort, investment and time. Thus, if the idea is not good enough in terms of "New Value created", it should be junked and the innovator needs to go back to the creative idea stage and generate a more valuable idea.

Determining the value of an Idea

The value of an idea is determined by the range of needs it satisfies, the number of needs it uniquely satisfies, the number of unsatisfied needs it satisfies and the cost at which it satisfies these needs. If the idea satisfies a larger range of needs at a lower cost in comparison to the existing products, the creative idea is valuable and is worthy of taking to the next step in the Innovation Development Process, namely 3D designing.

Idea Value = f(Range of needs, Depth of needs)

Principle of 'New Value Creation': The principle of new value creation is at the heart of innovation. This principle is so central to an innovation such that without its application a new entity is not categorised as an innovation.

Case : CIPLA

Cipla successfully opposed the grant of a patent to Boehringer for Tiotropium Bromide Monohydrate branded as Spiriva. This is utilised in inhalers. The patent was successfully opposed on the basis that it did not enhance therapeutic efficacy. Thus, enhancement of therapeutic efficacy is critical for the product to be recognised as an innovation for the process of granting a patent.

Integration of the principle of 'New Value Creation' in Patent Law: This principle is enshrined in Patent Law in terms of an exception to patentability under Sec.3(d) of the Indian Patents Act. Sec. 3(d) of the Act ensures that only those product innovations that demonstrate increased effectiveness are patentable. Change in form is insufficient for patentability.

Sec. 3 of the Indian Patents Act, 1970

What are not inventions

(d) the mere discovery of a new form of a known substance which does not result in the enhancement of the known efficacy of that substance or the mere discovery of any new property or new use for a known substance or of the mere use of a known process, machine or apparatus unless such known process results in a new product or employs at least one new reactant.

Explanation: For the purposes of this clause, salts, esters, ethers, polymorphs, metabolites, pure form, particle size, isomers, mixtures of isomers, complexes, combinations and other derivatives of known substance shall be considered to be the same substance, unless they differ significantly in properties with regard to efficacy; The phrase 'Enhancement of the known efficacy' specified in Sec.3(d) integrates the aforementioned principle in Patent Law.

Value Mutation

This is a skill which needs to be applied by the innovator at the 'Value Analysis' stage in the Innovation Development Process. The objective of the application of this skill is to enhance the inherent value in the innovation idea in order to make it feasible.

More often than not, we reject ideas on the basis of 'Why they won't work?' or 'What is wrong with them?' In the process, we also destroy the 'Value' in the idea.

Let us examine this from the angle of an 'Idea Value Scale'.

Even if 90% of an idea is valueless and impractical, our rejection of the idea also destroys the 'Value' in the 'Idea'. Along with the bath water, we also throw the baby away.

We need to retain the value part of the idea, while at the same time, we need to eliminate the valueless part of the idea. This can be done smoothly by using our judgement positively in order to 'Extract value' out of perspectives or knowledge domains which are different from ours. Extracting value can be utilised by an Innovator to form a new perception or to mutate the current perception. On applying extracting value, invariably, the solution improves.

Value mutation: The application of the skill of extracting value results in idea evolution, enhancement and development.

The innovator needs to use this skill continually but its most critical application is in reference to feedback from critical stakeholders of the proposed innovation.

When the innovator exposes the proposed innovation to critical stakeholders such as users, process managers and intermediaries, there is a tendency for the innovator to display a defensive attitude towards the innovation and its attributes. This blocks the evolution of the proposed innovation into a more robust solution. An Innovator tends to fall in love with his creation. Then he/she develops blind spots and is not able to see its limitations. Therefore defensiveness of the innovator is counter-productive. At this stage the innovator needs to utilise the skill of extracting value in order to extract the value out of the feedback and suggestions given by the stakeholders and incorporate the value into the proposed innovation.

The objections raised by the audience are in effect, "Opportunities" for enhancing the value in the proposed innovation. The Innovator needs to extract the value out of these objections and build it into the proposed innovation.This effort invested in idea development is not wasted. It invariably improves the innovative solution, thereby reducing the risk of failure. Thus extracting value enables 'Value mutation'. An original idea with a lot of impractical overtones and impossibilities can change into a workable and feasible idea through the process of extracting value and development. Thus, the skill of extracting value builds flexibility in the process of creation which is crucial to the process of generating a successful innovation.

Applications of Extracting Value

1. Prototype failure

When a prototype fails, the innovator needs to examine with a magnifying glass:

- What worked?
- What part of the solution worked?
- What feature of the solution created new value?
- Which feature worked?

The answer to these questions would be the value that

would need to be integrated into the prototype redesign. Invariably the new design would be more workable and feasible in comparison to the tested prototype.

2. Ideation within constraints

Almost everybody thinks that they cannot innovate because they have a lot of constraints. Who does not have constraints? Constraints are in fact opportunities to design something completely new as well as feasible. In this context let us examine the mythological story of "Prahlad".

Mythological Story of Prahlad

There was king called Hrinkshyap. He was evil. He worshiped the creator "Brahma"and undertook great penance in order to please him. Brahma appeared before him a and granted him a wish. Hrinkshyap wanted to be someone who can never be defeated. So the wish that he asked for was, 'No man, woman or animal should be able to kill me, neither I should be killed at home nor outside, neither in the morning nor at night, neither with a hand held weapon nor with a hand released weapon'. Brahma granted the wish. So, Hrinkshyap became arrogant and cruel.

> **Constraints**
> -Cannot be killed by man, woman or animal
> -Cannot be killed at night or during the day
> -Cannot be killed by a hand held weapon or by a hand released weapon

Thus, the constraints were phenomenal. However, this did not deter the preserver GOD 'Vishnu' to take the form of 'Narsingh' to kill him. The form of 'Narsingh' was a creation within all the constraints of the wish granted by Brahma. Thus, constraints are in fact great opportunities to create something entirely new. Constraints become blocks when we cease to practice flexibility in the process of idea creation.

Case: Just-in-time retail

This constraints-based innovation is visible in the just-in-time process innovation implemented by Japanese small retailers. These retailers were extremely cramped for space. There was no space of keeping any inventory at the retail outlet. So, they designed the supply chain process to ensure that that goods are supplied just-in time to replenish the items getting sold. This not only enhanced the utilisation of retail space available, it also reduced the inventory costs.

Case: Square watermelons

Watermelons, as they usually grow take an oval shape. This is a terrible constraint for transportation as well as storage because the volume of space occupied is larger than the mass of the watermelons. The constraint is the over-all volume of space available in the transportation vehicle. So, an innovative farmer grew square shaped watermelons. He put a square box over the nascent watermelons. As the watermelons grew, they took the shape of the box. The transportation vehicle could now carry approximately 20% more watermelons. Thus, there is infinite value which can be created within constraints. When we identify and give shape to this value, we can innovate within constraints.

Process Innovation Fusion with IT

Process Innovation

Organisations are a sum total of processes. These processes are the basis of organisational effectiveness and efficiency. Industrial engineering symbols have been utilised for the purpose of process innovation in most organisations. However, the application has been more on shop floor processes rather than management processes. In management processes the opportunity for innovation remains largely untapped.

This opportunity has further been multiplied by the frequency of technology shifts happening in Information Technology.

Thus, fusion with IT is a major source of process innovation. However, we need to be careful that process wastage is removed before IT is fused into the process. If that is not done, the benefits of IT fusion shall be muted.

Case: Dam site design flaw

In a Hydro electric power corporation engaged in dam

construction, a design flaw is discovered at the dam site. The rectification process is mapped below:

Symbols used for process mapping: The symbols used are industrial engineering symbols. These are standardised the world over for mapping processes.

Process Element	Industrial Engineering symbol
Operation	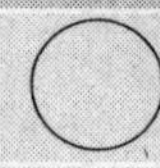
Inspection	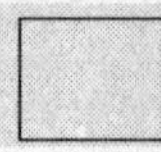
Delay	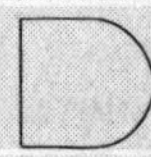
Transport	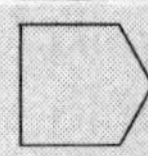
Storage	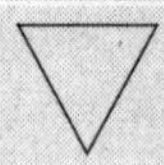

On utilising these symbols, we can map and analyse any process in an organisation on the basis of quality, cost and time.

Step 1: Current process of rectifying design flaw discovered at dam site

Process Assessment
Parameters
Quality Cost Time

Process map: Dam site design flaw removal

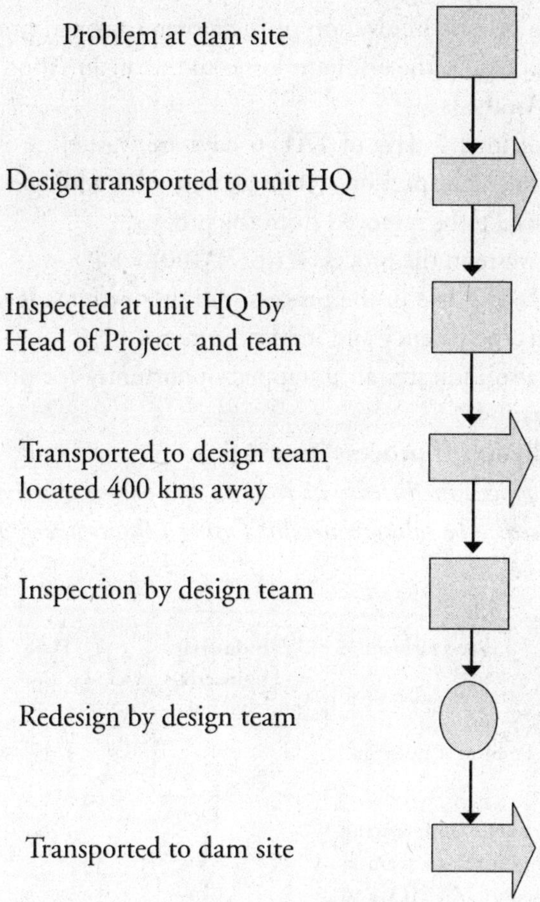

(Turn Around Time)=7 days

The loss to the company for every day of delay is 30 lakhs. Therefore, the total loss to the organisation due to the design flaw is 210 lakhs.

It would be highly beneficial for the organisation to undertake process innovation of the aforementioned process in order to reduce the resultant losses to the organisation.

Process Analysis

- Out of total 7 days of TAT, 6 days are wasted in either travelling or inspection. These are non-value adding events and need to be removed from the process.
- % of waste in the process = ((6/7)*100) = 84%
- The % of waste in the process indicates extreme level of process inefficiency and ineffectiveness.
- This also indicates an untapped opportunity for process innovation.

The challenge of process innovation

How can process inefficiency be reduced and process effectiveness be enhanced? The solution lies in 'Fusing IT into the process'.

Process Innovation

S.No	Process element	Industrial Engineering Symbol	Time
1	Problem at Dam Site	□	1 day
2	Video conferencing with design team at company HQ and joint redesigning.	○	1 day
		TAT	2 days

Impact

- Enhancement of process efficiency by 350%.
- Reduced costs to the organisation to the tune of 5 * 30 = 150 lakhs.

These kind of opportunities for process innovation abound in organisations because the frequency of technology shifts in IT has been high. Each and every one of these technology shifts has unleashed opportunities for process innovation.

The struggle for providing better services and at lower cost continues to subsist. Process innovation enables us to achieve this objective.

Case: T &D Course delivery in Joan Institute of Management

In the MBA course of Joan Institute of Management, the T&D course was done in the second year by the students.

Training process (costing/class)

S.No	Process element	Cost
1	Perception expansion through PPT presentation	nil
2	Application exercise	nil
3	Case studies on paper (10 cases * 5 pages	50

Total number of courses: **10**
Number of classes per course: **2**
Average number of students per class: **25**
Cost of paper per semester: **25*2*10*50=25000**

Process Innovation

S.no	Process Element	Cost
1	PPT presentation	Nil
2	Application exercises	Nil
3	*Deployment of Virtual Learning Environment* • *Loading of cases,presentations and assignments on the VLE*	Negligible (Domain and webspace already paid for by the institute)

Impact

- Cost reduction: 25000/semester

Benefits

- Students: 24x7 availability of learning material on the VLE. Professors: Additional communication platform with the students. Learning: Enhanced
- Benefit to cost analysis i.e. the value analysis indicates significant new value was created by the process innovation.

Success pattern of Process Innovations through 'Fusion with IT'

The success pattern of process innovations through fusion with IT is strikingly clear on the basis of the following wide spread successes:

- On line Banking
- On line transfer of funds to accounts in other banks (NEFT)
- On line railway ticketing system

- On line retail
- On line payment of taxes and the submission of tax return forms. (Service Tax, Income Tax)

Extension of this Success Pattern

The potential for multiplicative extension of the aforementioned success pattern is infinite as organised work life rotates around organisational systems and processes.

Systems Innovation

One of the key challenges that any reformer faces is "How to change the System?"

People rebel against the prevailing system but subsequently when they are at the helm of affairs, they too become a part of the system and are unable to reform or harness the system. In fact, the system tames them to its own behaviour.

How is this challenge to be dealt with? Or are we always going to be weaker than the system? Is the system always going to rule us or do we have the ways and means of taming and changing the system?

What is a system?

A system consists of a set of processes which work together to convert an input into a desired output.Therefore, what is the challenge of systemic innovation?

System Innovation consists of process innovation in multiple processes which constitute the system. Thus, the challenge of system innovation is bigger in comparison to process innovation.

Case: Training System innovation in B Systems

Step 1: Mapping the Training System in B Systems

The map of a system will consist of all the processes that constitute the system. The key processes in the training system are assimilated below:

- TNA
- Learner analysis
- Instruction design
- Training delivery
- Training metrics

System MapDMP
(Training System)
Training Needs Analysis (TNA)
Learner analysis
Instruction design
Training delivery
Metrics

Step 2: Fusing IT into every process

S.No	Process	Fusion element(IT)
1	TNA	Mobile based App.
2	Learner analysis	Excel based learner analaysis to be filled by each learner.
3	Instruction Design	• Virtual learning environment modules focused on • Perception expansion • Assimilation • Applications • Analysis and synthesis.
4	Training delivery	• Two learning platforms • Mobile based App. • VLE

5	Training metrics for measuring training effectiveness	• Training App based Form submission • Training Database • Integration and consolidation of training metrics • Setting of quality levels • Identification of errors

The integration of these aforementioned processes resulted in 'Systemic Innovation' in the training function of B Systems.

This kind of systemic innovation is the requirement from every leader who wishes to make any kind of lasting change.

Case: Primary Years Program (PYP) in IB Schools (International Bacclaureate)

IB schools have brought about systemic innovation in the School Education System.

The school education system consists of multiple processes which interact and integrate to form a system. The IB education system is a systemic innovation over the traditional education systems which focus on rote learning and regurgitation in exams.

How is the IB educational system a systemic innovation?

Processes	Traditional educational system	IB School System
Learning Process	• Rote learning • Outside-in	• Inquiry based learning • Inside-out
Assessment and feedback to students	Paper based	Internet based
Feedback to parents	Parent teacher meetings	• Newsletter through e-mail • Parent teacher meetings
Learning content	Book	Internet + Book
Facilitation of learning	Individual assimilation of learning	• Group exercises • Individual graphic organisers • Individual assimilation
Intelligence developed	Memory focused	Thinking focused
Learning catalysts	Book	Inquiry process, Ability to learn
Educational focus	Learning	Competency
Learning achieved	Short term	Long term
Learning locus	Content centered	Learner centered

In the IB system, there is process innovation in reference to multiple processes that constitute the educational system. Hence, it is an example of system innovation. System Mapping consists of identifying the multiple processes that constitute the system, categorising them into core and peripheral processes and synthesising the qualitative or quantitative value created by each process.

System Map

Processes	Value created
P1	V1
P2	V2
	Total value created by the system

Core Process: P1 Peripheral Process: P2

The processes can be categorised as 'Core' or 'Peripheral'. As we innovate on multiple processes thereby enhancing the total value created, we enter the realm of system innovation.

Process of Systemic innovation'

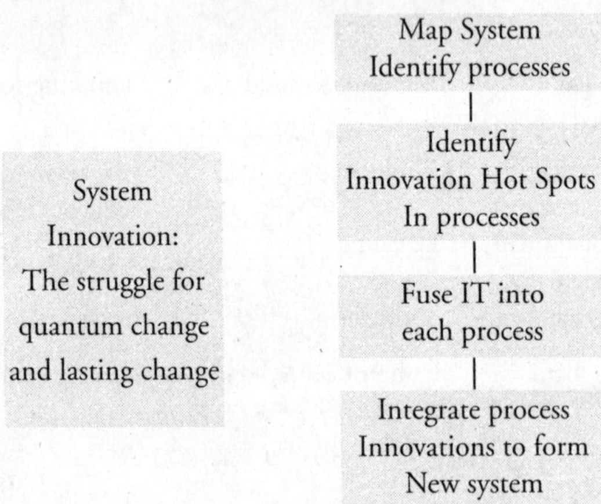

Case: E-filing system of court cases in Delhi High Court.

The E-filing system of court cases is a typical example of system innovation using IT. The impact has been significant.

The system map for court case filing is mapped below:

Case filing system

Process 1: Identification of petition/appeal/case category
Process 2: Formulation of petition/appeal/pleading
Process 3: Formulation of affidavit and vetting by oath commmissioner
Process 4: Attaching of evidence in the form of documents as annexures
Process 5: Attaching of vakalatnama
Process 6: Buying and attaching of court fees stamps
Process 7: Attaching of prescribed forms for the case category(if any)
Process 8: Filing of petition in the court registry
Process 9: Removal of errors in the petition.

System Innovation: E-filing

Process 1: Establishment of efiling centres
Process 2:Registration of advocate/petitioner
Process 3: Utilization of html/XML forms for inputting case data
Process 4: Converting pleading and documents into an integrated pdf file with indexing.
Process 5: On-line purchasing of estamps and linking them to the pleading.
Process 6: Feedback through e-mail.
Process 7: On-line intimation and rectification of errors

Process 8: Retention of original documents with the pleader for the court's reference.

Process 9: Intimations through sms/e-mail regarding case registration/listing/process fee.

Fusion of the case filing system with IT

On fusing IT elements into the aforementioned processes the manual case filing system got converted into an e-filing system which brought about a significant change in its effectiveness and efficiency

System	IT elements for fusion
Process 1: Identification of petition/appeal/case category	• E-mail • Pdf format • Digital signature • Forms • Cloud • Database • Cyber Security • Bar coding
Process 2: Formulation of petition/appeal/pleading	
Process 3: Formulation of affidavit and vetting by oath commissioner	
Process 4: Attaching of evidence in the form of documents as annexures	
Process 5: Attaching of vakalatnama	
Process 6: Buying and attaching of court fees stamps	
Process 7: Attaching of prescribed forms for the case category(if any)	
Process 8: Filing of petition in the court registry	
Process 9: Removal of errors in the petition	

Application of e-filing system

Initially the e-filing system was only for tax matters. Later on it was extended to organizational,arbitration and constitutional matters.

Impact:

Year	Cases filed through e-filing
2013	609
2014-15	11252
2015-16	18258

The rising number of cases filed through the efiling system indicates the new value created by the e-filing system for the litigant. It has also created new value for the court.

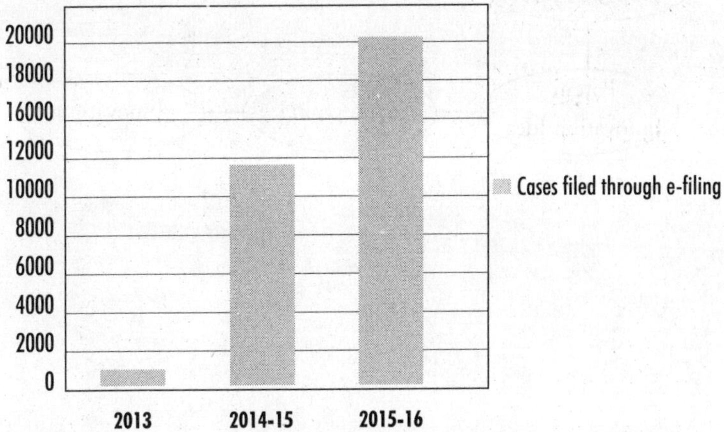

The potential of saving in terms of space required for storage of case files is huge. The space required was reduced from 2 lakh square feet to 6 square feet. Hence this is a successful case of system innovation.

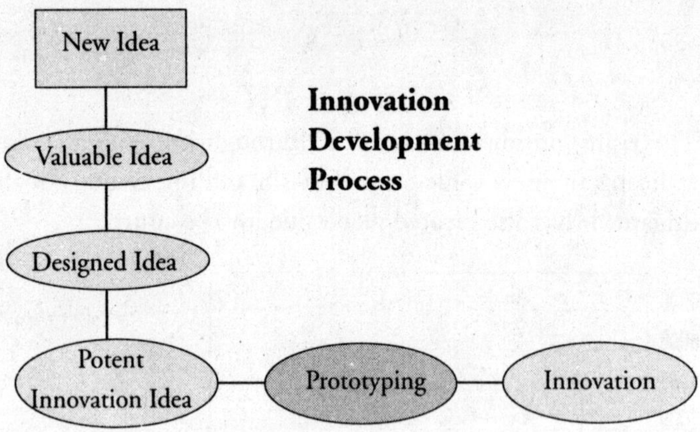

Innovation Development Process

Prototyping

A critical step in the Innovation Development process is prototyping. If an Innovator chooses to skip this step, the consequences can be disastrous. It bridges the gap between a 'good concept' and a 'proven working model'. It enables design improvements at low costs. In case, prototyping is not done, our innovation endeavour would have a tendency to result in disaster, thereby destroying capital rather than creating it.

Prototyping refers to the conversion of the potent innovation idea into a working model. In the case of a process and system innovation, it refers to paper prototyping followed by its implementation in parallel to the existing system. In case of a marketing innovation such as a 'New Sales promotion scheme' or a 'New Dealer motivation strategy', it refers to the implementation of the Innovation in one area. In the case of product innovation, it refers to the creation of a working model in order to test its efficacy.

The advantages of prototyping are multiple. Prototyping provides data to the innovator regarding the effectiveness of the innovation; the user needs it satisfies; the benefits and costs vis-a-vis competing products/processes. This data can be utilised by the innovator to get the innovation accepted by collaborators and users.

Without this data, the resistance to the innovator would be insurmountable. Prototyping is a source of invaluable learning to the innovator. 'Innovation ideas' which look great at the 'Potent new idea' stage tend to loose their lustre and charm at the 'Prototype stage'. One look at the prototypes and the concept which looked so charming at the initial stages gets automatically rejected.

The reverse of this phenomenon is also true. The resistance to a concept tends to disappear, if the prototype performs better than the existing products.

The innovator needs to put the prototype in the hands of the user and observe the interaction between the prototype and the user. This yields further insights into improvement opportunities. The objections raised by the user can be used as opportunities for further innovations. Wherever possible, the innovator should demonstrate the prototype in parallel to the existing product.

System Prototyping

Process innovations in the value chain have a cascading impact on all organisation success factors. However, if the 'Proof of concept' is missing, nobody in the organisation is going to accept that there is a better way of doing things. Therefore, system prototyping plays a vital part in the development and acceptance of Process Innovations. A low cost system of system prototyping is called "Human and Paper simulations".

Paper and Human Simulations:

This involves simulating the entire process using 'Paper' and 'Humans', in an open area.

Case: Customer ordering system through ATMs

Step1: The customer interface screens are made on paper utilising the same specifications in terms of size and colour as would finally be prevalent.

Step2: A 'Human' plays the role of the ATM. The Human-ATM is briefed about the responses in terms of "Screens" which need to be shown to the customer in response to specific buttons pressed by the customer. The screen responses of the system in terms of if-then statements are designed and given to the human-ATM.

Step3: The flow of 'Data' from the input screens to the backend Database systems is simulated using 'Humans as Data carriers'.

Step4: The backend database is also simulated by a human who takes data from the 'Human Data Carrier', processes/ stores data and also provides output in terms of reports to different stakeholders inclusive of 'customers' and '"decision making personnel'.

Step 5: An actual customer, without any specific briefing about the system is called in and asked to 'use the system'.

Step 6: The Innovator observes the following points: The customer's reactions to the system dynamics. This includes the colour scheme and data sizes of the customer Interface screens. The innovator should also interact with the customer and assimilate met/unmet expectations from the system, system gaps and system effectiveness. On the basis of these observations, the innovator can change the requisite process (es) at no cost and observe the new process in action.

Step 7: After the removal of "Process glitches through Paper and Human simulation", he needs to implement the Innovated process in one place in parallel to the existing process. This would provide an opportunity to collect process effectiveness and efficiency data. This data would be critical in getting the process innovation accepted for cascading in the organisation.

The utility of 'Paper & Human Simulation' is that it enables the observation of the functioning of the entire system as well as each of its components at zero cost. Thus, either the entire system or any of the components can easily be redesigned and the resistance to redesigning would be minimal. The demonstration of the process simulation can also be utilised to get the acceptance of the actual users and stakeholders of the system. When System simulation is done in this manner, the glitches in the process get removed, thereby reducing the number of repeat prototypes that would need to be done.

Product Prototyping

Case: Product display innovation

At the retail point, the Dominant Mental Pattern of product displays is that they are organised on the walls or on the counter. On challenging this DMP, we get the perspective of utilising the ceiling for product displays. Fusing product display requirement with a hanging light, we get the idea of products displayed on a circular light

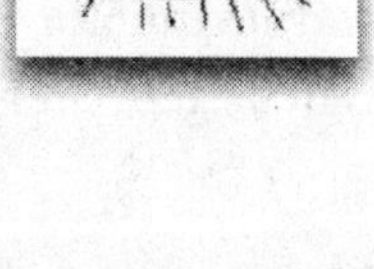

hanging from the ceiling of the retail point.

The design of the proposed innovation is given in the accompanying diagram

Low Cost prototyping

Converting the design into a working prototype is critical in the innovation development process. A large number of product innovation ideas die because of the huge energy required to convert them into working prototypes. A low cost prototyping strategy is to segregate the product into its components. These are:

- Hanging wire
- Spring
- Plastic half dome with hangers
- Bulb holder
- LED Bulb

After identifying the specifications of each of these components, the innovator needs to source them and then find vendors for each component. These can be assembled by the innovator into working prototypes.

If the prototypes work and create the additional value envisaged at the raw idea stage, the prototypes can be categorised and rolled out as innovations.

Low Cost Prototyping strategy

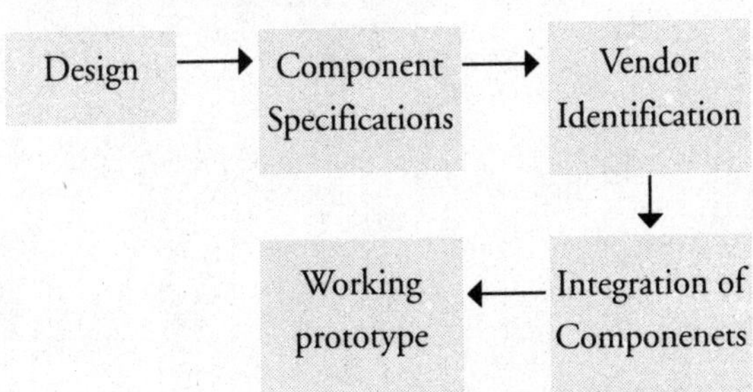

Case: Prototyping in auto companies

In auto companies due to the huge risk involved in new product launches, multiple kinds of prototypes are made before the product is approved for launching.

The different kinds of prototypes in their sequence of prototyping are mapped below:

Mechanical Prototype
(Structural and packaging)

↓

Engineering Prototype
(Soft tools,line trials & validation)

↓

Verification Prototype
(Hard tools & validation)

↓

Production Prototype
(Pilot Batch & sign off on all processes)

Success and Failure Pattern

Around us, we see successful innovations being highlighted. We also see the carcasses of numerous innovation attempts.

Is there a pattern of innovation success or failure? In order to innovate successfully, we need to learn from the numerous attempts which succeeded or failed so that we don't repeat the mistakes already committed. So, let's map the success or failure pattern that exists underneath successful or failed innovations.

Cases : Ceasefire and Vacuumiser

'Cease fire', was a small Fire extinguisher with car, home and office applications and 'Vacuumizer', was a product used for increasing the longevity of food items. Both the products were innovations created by the same organisation, yet one succeeded and the other failed.

Cease Fire: Pattern of Success

Cease fire was a success resulting in rising fortunes of the innovating organisation, to the extent that the 'Cease

fire Success' was often quoted in management circles. Conversely, vacuumizer was a failure. High inventory levels accompanied with minimum sales were the undoing of the company.

What is the underlying success and failure pattern?

Cease Fire succeeded because of the following factors:

1.Unique Needs Satisfaction

1.1 Ease of Usage

1.2 Easy to store

1.3 Easily accessible at the time of need

1.4 Protection from being burnt

1.5 Display of 'Concern'

The standard "Fire extinguishers" are heavy, huge, difficult to use and have different systems of use. The difficulty level can be ascertained by the fact that one needs to attend a training program to use them properly.

2. Costly Alternatives

The costs of alternative standard fire extinguishers were higher than those of "Cease Fire".

3. Wide Availability

The marketing of standard extinguishers was fundamentally aimed at industrial users. Hence, selling and marketing systems were aligned to industrial buyers.

Therefore, even if a consumer wanted to purchase a standard extinguisher, he/she would find it difficult to locate a seller at the first place, and subsequently additional costs would have to be incurred to get it to one's residence. Cease fire, on the other hand was marketed directly to the consumer, the house or office. The wide availability of the product along with ease of purchase turned out to be a significant success pattern.

Vacuumizer: Pattern of failure

After the success of 'Cease fire', the organisation launched 'Vacuumizer' , another innovation. However, it was a complete failure.

What was the pattern of failure?

On the surface, it seemed to have the same success parameters in terms of wide availability and needs satisfaction.

The product function was to keep the food fresh. Thus people could use it as a tiffin if required.However, on close analysis, we observe that no unique needs were being satisfied by the product. The need was not strong enough to warrant the purchase of 'vacuumizer'. 'Fridge' satisfies the same need of the 'longevity' of food items.

Fridge also satisfies some more needs such as cooling of water and ice formation among other things. Additionally, fridge is an accepted paradigm in the consumer's mind while 'vacuumizer' is unknown. Therefore, vacuumizer failed because the alternative systems of satisfying the same consumer needs were better in terms of range of needs satisfied along with paradigm acceptance in the target market.

Parameters for selecting potent innovation ideas

On analysing the aforementioned cases, we can synthesise a 'Set of Parameters' for selecting, 'Potent Innovation Ideas'. This would help us decide, whether a particular innovation is worthy of further investment in terms of resources. Such a tool would be valuable for its ability to ascertain the viability of an innovation. This set of parameters is titled 'Innovator's Sieve'.

Innovator's Sieve

B:Benefits C:Costs

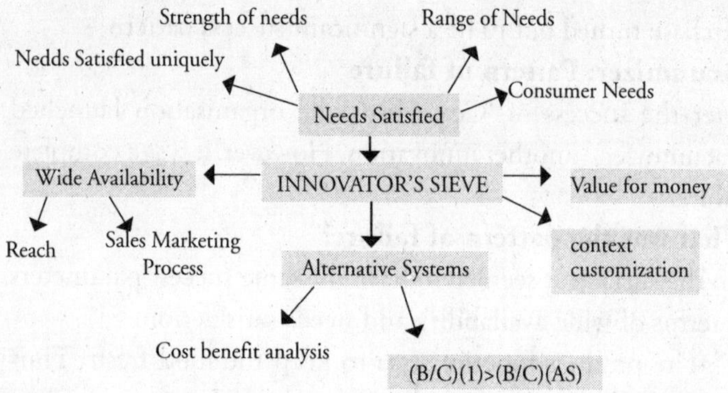

The innovator's sieve consists of the following parameters:

1. (Benefits/Cost)Innovation>(Benefits/Cost)Alternative systems: This is the measure of the value of the product to its users. It is the most pertinent of the factors in the innovator's sieve. The value differential between the innovation and its competing products determines the success of the innovation.

2.Range of needs satisfied: If the range of needs satisfied includes some unique needs which are not currently being satisfied by any alternative product, then the probability of success of the innovation multiplies. The range of needs satisfied and the strength of the needs are key determiners of the success of the innovation.

3.Context customisation:

This is a measure of the adaptability of the innovation to the working environment of the user. A lot of innovations fail because they do not integrate with the other systems at the workplace of the user.

4. Marketing and marketing communication:

An innovation not marketed well has a tendency to go into oblivion without seeing the light of day. Thus, innovation value is lost and a lot of effort is wasted in vain because it is never perceived by the user.

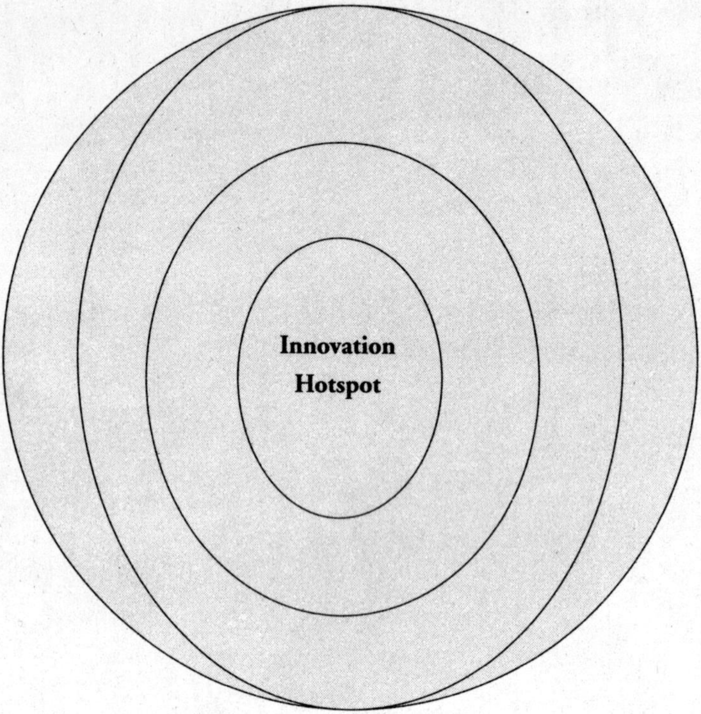
Innovation
Hotspot

Innovation Hotspots

Innovation: Where? That is one of the fundamental questions that we set out to answer when we started this book.Now we shall answer that question by identifying innovation hotspots within a firm.

The identification of innovation hotspots constitutes the formulation of, 'Innovation Strategy'. The success of an innovation is determined by its visibility and its impact as a multiplier. Innovation is possible at every operational point in the organisation. However, in order to gain the maximum from an innovation effort, we need to choose those innovation sensitive areas which will have the maximum impact on the total value created for the external or the internal customer.

These innovation sensitive areas are called innovation hotspots. 'Identifying innovation hotspots and deploying the innovation ecosystem to develop innovations in these innovation hotspots constitutes the', 'Innovation Strategy' of the firm. Innovation requires a large amount of intense effort. No point pursuing it, if it is not going to create even a ripple. Innovation creates a tidal wave. Even if one is not able to do that, at least a multiple ripple effect can be aspired for. This ripple effect is not going to be created, if one picks up areas randomly for innovation. The innovation hot spots in an organisation are found in the value chain. Even within the value chain there are certain areas in which an innovation would have a quantum impact on the quality of output. Every department also has a value chain and certain elements in the value chain have a bigger impact on the output in comparison to others. These elements can be categorised as 'Innovation Hotspots'.

Organisations that have not identified innovation hotspots would be prone to not getting a substantial return on investment w.r.t. the time and resources invested in the innovation projects.

Case: Innovation Hotspots in the paint shop of an auto company.

The operational process in the paint shop of a car manufacturer is mapped below:

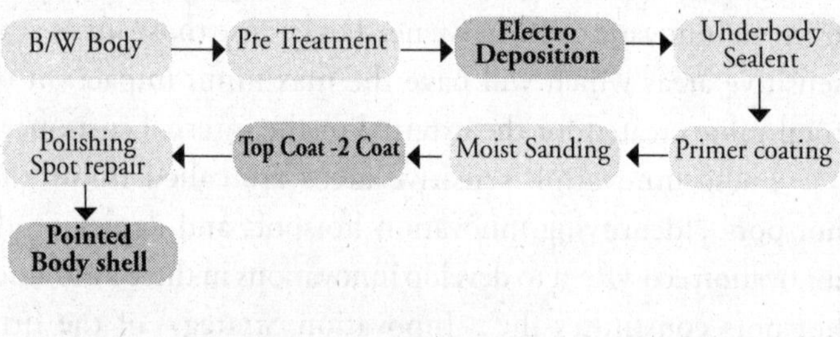

In this operational process, innovation is possible at every element in the process. However, in case we innovate in the process elements of 'Electro-Deposition' and 'Top Coat', the value differential created is maximum.

Hence, these are known as Innovation Hotspots.

Criteria for Innovation Hotspot Selection

- Operating cost (Direct and Indirect material cost)
- Work content (Repair cost on down stream process–Polishing, Spot repair)
- Process complication (skilled manpower required)
- Productivity (meeting target schedule)
- Reduce non value addition activity
- Reducing energy consumption
- Frequency of technology shifts

Case: Coal based power producer

There are innovation sensitive areas at corporate level, unit level as well as departmental level.

Innovation Sensitive Areas at Corporate Level

- Ash disposal
- Design
    - Maintainability aspects examination at the time of design
    - Review of design margins and layout
    - Standardisation of power plant equipment
- Water plus and carbon negative approach
- Fuel availability:
    - Quality and quantity
    - Fuel switch and mixing
- Sustained PLF>95%
- Sale of un-requisitioned power
- Cost of engineering

Innovation Sensitive Areas at Unit level

- Inventory control at the unit level
- Procurement systems
- Emission control
- Maintenance

Case: Sales department in FMCG Company

Can there be any innovation sensitive areas in the sales process of an FMCG company?

Those elements in the sales process which will have the maximum impact on sales are Innovation Hotspots in sales.The innovation Hotspots identified by an FMCG company are as follows:

- Bazaar presence
- Dealer motivation
- In-shop visibility
- Sales in malls

Case: Design Department

The design department cascades value into all the downstream processes. Hence, an innovation in the design department has a significant and far reaching impact on the total value created. Within the design process, an innovation at a key process element will create a multiplier impact on the value created by the design department. The value chain and the requisite innovation sensitive area are given below:

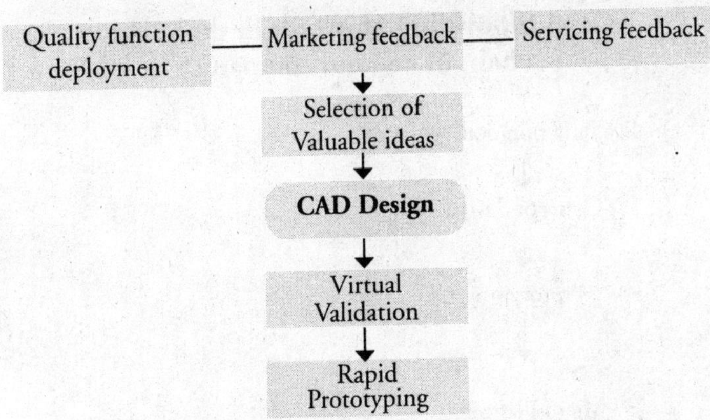

Case: IT department of FMCG manufacturer

The innovation sensitive areas identifiedby the IT department of a FMCG company are given below:

- Business processes
- Collections
- Vendor collaboration
- Supply chain management

Case: Innovation hotspots for a BPO

- Recruitment:
  - Employee referrals
- Employee engagement:
  - Metrics
- Competency development
  - Mobile app-based.
  - Training material

Case: Innovation Hotspots in the value chain of an auto company

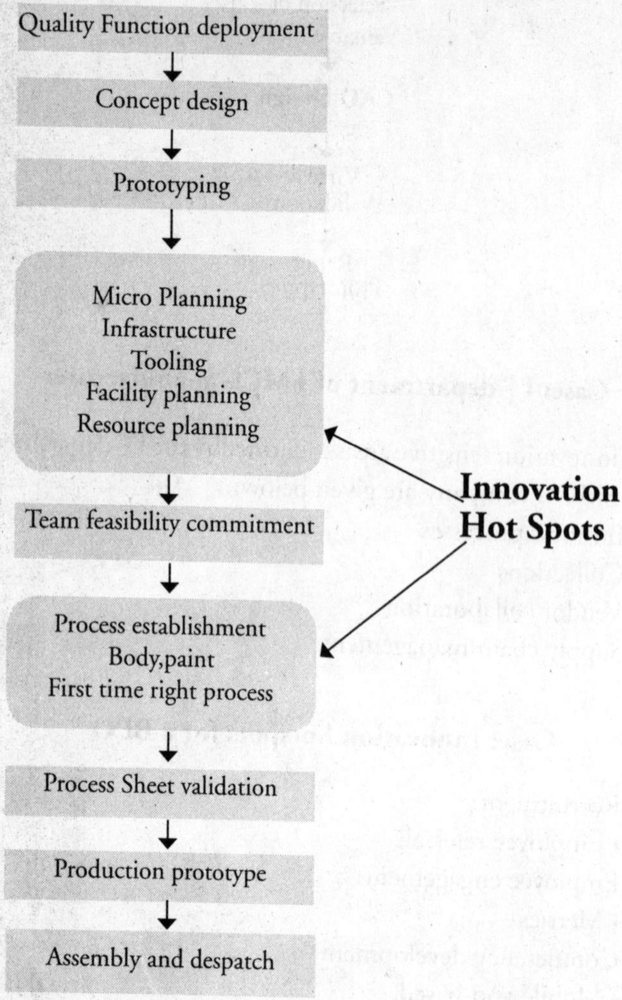

Case: Telecom Technology provider Strategic innovation hotspots

This telecom technology provider was functioning in a highly volatile business environment with numerous competitors as well as technology shifts. In this situation, it became imperative for the organisation to identify and prioritise the strategic innovation hotspots that would give the organisation a decisive edge. The strategic innovation hotspots identified by the organisation are given below:

- Mobile Virtual Network Operator (MVNO)
- Intelligent infrastructure for communities
- Convergence of devices
- Telecom network optimisation on the basis of demand

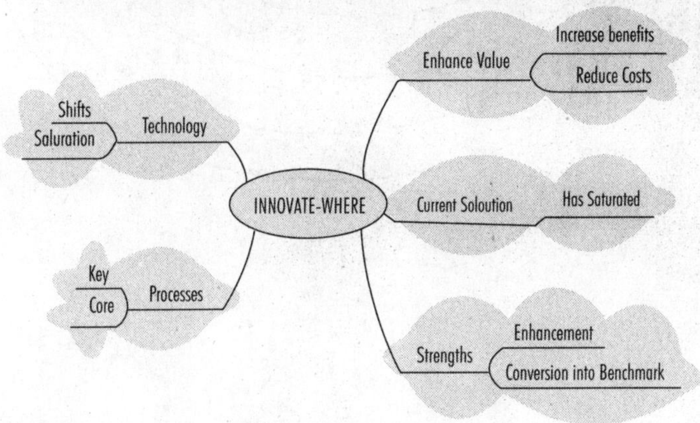

Elements of the , 'Innovation Strategy' for a firm:

- Identification of innovation Hotspots.
- Deployment of the innovation ecosystem for the identified innovation hotspots.

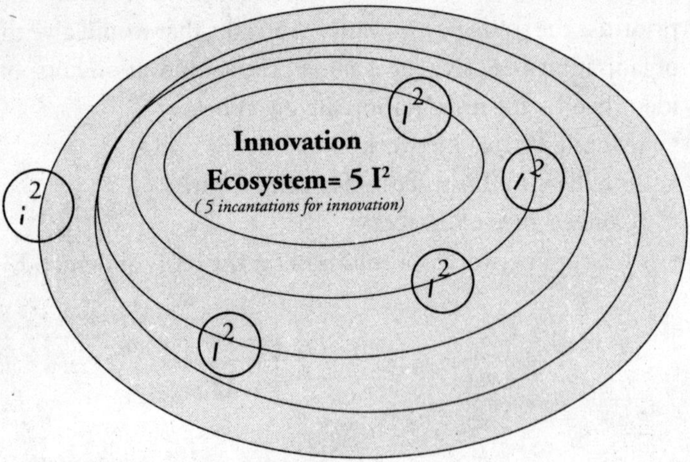
Innovation
Ecosystem= 5 I²
(5 incantations for innovation)

Innovation Ecosystem

The key questions that comes to the mind are 'What is an Ecosystem?' and 'why do we need an Innovation Ecosystem?' An Ecosystem refers to a set of elements which dynamically work together to create a sustained output over a period of time. If any of the elements is missing the entire system fails. For example, The water cycle is a system that repeats itself year after year. If any of the elements of the system does not function, the system fails resulting in drought or floods.

Application to Innovation: Innovation is the output of an organisational system. If the different elements of this organisational system are not put into place then the system does not function and the desired innovation output would not happen and even if it does happen, it will be sporadic without any consistency.

The Organisational Challenge

Innovations in organisations are usually flashes in the pan. They are the result of unusual perseverance and initiative on the part of the innovator. These flashes are difficult to sustain.

However, innovations are the life and blood of an organisation which enable it to sustain and grow.

Therefore each and every organisation faces the challenge, "How do we enable a continuous flow of innovation?"

Most organisations have viewed this challenge simplistically. They feel that conducting a workshop on 'innovation' will enable the organisational personnel to generate innovations.

Case: An innovative FMCG company

This FMCG company was known for its innovative products and organisational processes. After conducting an organisational diagnosis, the organisation discovered that though its products were innovative, the sales process lacked innovation.

Therefore, it decided to tackle this problem by conducting a training program on 'Innovation' for key sales personnel along with identification of innovation hot spots of 'In-shop visibility' and 'productivity of distributor salesman'.

The approach of the organisation is mapped below:

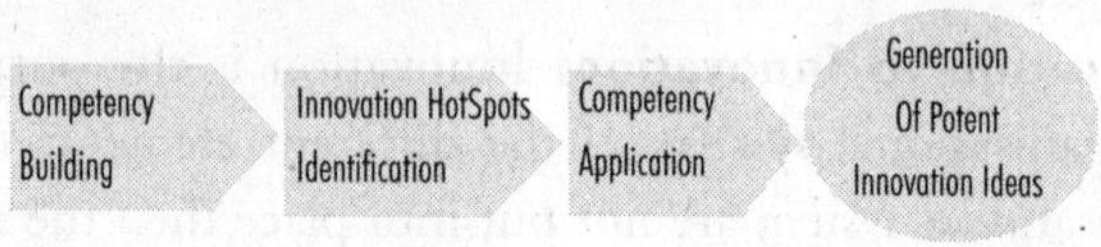

Dynamics unleashed:The organisation had entrenched values related to innovation. The training program was received very enthusiastically by the sales team. The sales team applied itself to generate potent innovation ideas in the identified innovation hotspots. Multiple potent innovation ideas were generated. The workshop closed with an air of optimism about the future because of the imminent sales innovations which were bound to ensue.

Reality check after 4 months:

Not a single innovation could be implemented

Diagnostic Query: The organisation was puzzled by the result. Everything was all right. The workshop feedback was excellent. Why was there no deliverable result?

Diagnosis: The organisational blind spot lies in the absence of an 'Innovation EcoSystem'. Though competency development, innovation hotspot identification and competency application are elements of the innovation ecosystem, there are other elements of the innovation ecosystem which were not conceptualised by the organisation resulting in systemic failure.

Case: Telecom Company In dire straits

A telecom company was in dire straits because it was facing competition from larger players with greater financial and marketing capability. Therefore, the company focused on "Innovation in operations " in order to create a competitive edge. *The approach of the organisation for generating 'Innovation in operations'*

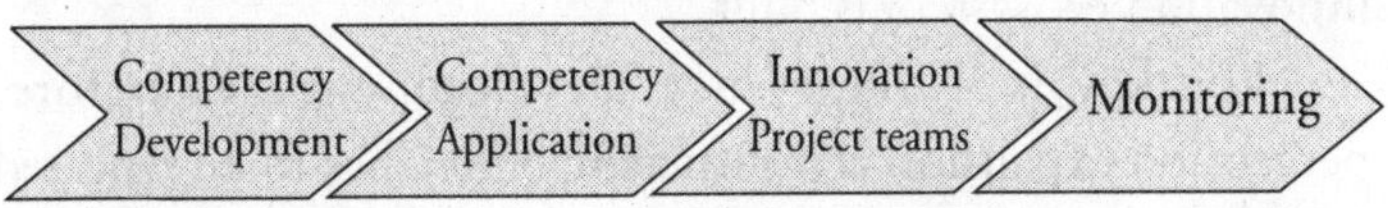

Diagnostic Query: Why did this organisation succeed while the earlier FMCG company failed in the innovation endeavour? Diagnosis:The different initiatives taken by the organisation constitute an 'Innovation Ecosystem'.

Difference in approaches of the FMCG co and the Telecom company:

The difference in the approaches of the two companies is illustrated below:

The FMCG company only concentrated on two elements of the innovation ecosystem which were insufficient for the generation of successful innovations because of the lack of focus on the innovation development process, the innovation support structures and progress review. The Telecom company on the other hand brought into play all the elements of the innovation ecosystem and hence the effort of the company bore fruit in terms of successful innovations.

This gives rise to the 'Innovation Ecosystem'.

The ecosystem consists of multiple processes which synergize and are interdependent on each other to create the output of innovation.

The Innovation Ecosystem

The Innovation Ecosystem consists of 5 Incantations for Innovation.

1: Innovation Competency Building

This consists of competency development of organisational personnel in the application of innovation tools, levers and processes. This is the foundation on which the rest of the innovation ecosystem is built.

The key is 'Competency Development'. Therefore, perception expansion is insufficient. There has to be repeated application of innovation tools and levers in order to catalyse innovation competency growth.

Incantation 2: Innovation Hotspots

Innovation Hotspots have to be identified in order to answer the often repeated question 'Where to innovate?'

Innovation hotspots are at the organisation, as well as at the departmental level. These innovation sensitive areas are the starting points of the innovation effort. It is indeed a sad story when the organisation spends 1 month in identifying the innovation sensitive area after constituting the innovation teams. This phenomenon indicates that the organisation does not understand the dynamics associated with innovation.

Incantation 3: Innovation Development Process

An application platform for the competency of innovation is the starting point of the innovation development process. An organisation cannot just develop the innovation competency and let the potential innovator meander in the unknown trails of innovation without any direction.

An application platform is a dedicated deployment of time in innovation teams in order to generate potent innovation ideas in the identified innovation hotspots.

This acts like the starting gun in the race on the road to innovation. The rest of the innovation development process from creative raw idea stage to potent innovation idea stage to prototyped idea stage to innovation has to be formalised by the organisation in order to enable repetitive and dependable utilisation by potential innovators.

Incantation 4: Innovation Support Structures

The innovator as well as the innovation development process needs to be nurtured and monitored in order to facilitate the resolution of problems which an innovator is bound to face on the path of innovation.

These innovation support structures include innovation mentors, innovation project budgets, availability of a wide set of technical competencies both within and outside the organisation and pecuniary as well as non-pecuniary incentives.

Incantation 5: Innovation Index Number

'If u want to manage something measure it, if you can't measure it, you can't manage it.' Therefore, measurement of the level of innovation generated by the innovation ecosystem of the organisation has to be done. The parameters for measurement include number of innovations generated, number of prototypes made and the number of potent innovation ideas approved for prototyping. A year on year innovation index number is a leading indicator of organisational profitability and success.

$5i^2$

5 incantations for innovation

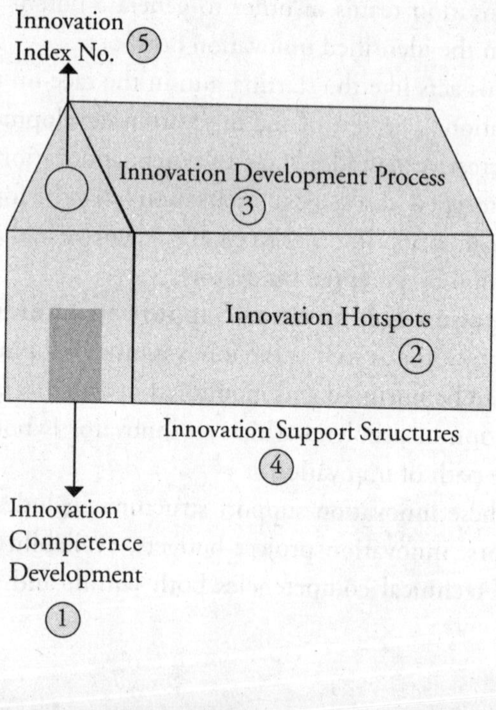

Case: Watch manufacturing company

A watch manufacturing company started operations in a market which was dominated by a public limited company having 75% market share along with product leadership.

This company in order to strengthen its presence started a slew of innovation initiatives.

Innovation Hotspots identified:

- New product cycle time: 50% of the industrial average
- Sales point and customer experience
- Technology shifts

Innovation Support Structures deployed:

- Task force/innovation hotspot
- Project budget
- Project mentor

Competency Building

- Training of task forces in innovation tools and the innovation development process.

Progress review:

- Progress review of the innovation teams and redeployment of team members.

Diagnosis: All the key elements of an innovation ecosystem were in place.

Impact: The organisation evolved into a strong brand, attained product leadership and also market leadership.

Case: Leading BPO

This leading BPO had innovation in its value system. It had global leadership ambitions. Thus, the HR head wanted to generate 'Innovations in HR'.

Innovation Sensitive Areas and Innovation Hotspots:
There were a myriad number of problems in some HR functions. Those were identified as 'Innovation Sensitive Areas'. Within each innovation sensitive area specific elements were identified as 'Innovation Hotspots'.

Innovation Sensitive Area	Innovation Hotspot
Competency Development	• Batch Size • Mobile app. based learning
Recruitment	• Applicant experience

Innovation Support Structure:

- Mentor
- Innovation Teams

Team and organisational dynamics:

The teams applied innovation tools and developed potent innovation ideas. They then took the feedback from different stakeholders and moved on to paper prototyping. The teams prototyped the input and output formats for the mobile app. to be utilised by different users of the system.

While this process was going on, the mentor left the organisation. This acted like a wet blanket on the innovation initiative and it quickly sank and vanished.

Diagnosis:

Though the different innovation initiatives required for the success of the innovation venture were put into place, the innovation ecosystem was not integrated into the organisational systems. If it had been so integrated, if one mentor left, the organisational dynamics would have automatically replaced him. Thus the approach of the organisation was singular rather than systemic. A focus on the 'Innovation Ecosystem' and the establishment of its operations would have ensured that an innovation initiative with such a high potential would not have perished so easily.

Case : Pharma company

This pharma company was at the point of launching a new product. The competing products were from companies which were well established in the product space with strong brands and deep advertising budgets. The pharma company was not in a position to compete with the established players in the area of advertising budgets.

The company then strategized to 'Innovate in Sales' in order to make the new product a success.

Innovation initiatives undertaken

- Innovation competency development of all sales teams
- Identification of innovation hotspots in Sales.
- Competency application forum
- Selection of 'Potent innovation ideas' for implementation
- Sales team leader as selector of innovations to be implemented
- Assimilation of successful sales innovations brought about by any team in a 'National Database of Sales Innovations' to be accessed by any other sales team for implementation.

Impact

- 75 successful innovations

Diagnosis

The innovation initiative was successful in generating the desired number of innovations. The reason is that the key elements required for the the functioning of the 'Innovation development process' were in place.

However, the frequency of the number of innovations would not sustain because of the lack of an innovation ecosystem. The initiative would succeed as a singular innovation initiative but the number of implemented innovations would fester out because the life and vibrancy of the innovation culture is dependent upon the innovation ecosystem. The innovation ecosystem designed in terms of the national database of innovations is too small and fragile for making a sustained impact on 'Innovation culture'.

Patenting

Patenting

On the path of innovation, what to do if one is able to reach the end of the tunnel? There is a huge amount of effort involved in the innovation development process and if one finally is successful after all the trials and tribulations, there would be enough vultures at the end of the tunnel to grab the successful innovation and claim it to be their own.

Therefore, an innovator needs to protect the fruit of the innovation endeavour through patenting.

This enables the patent holder i.e. the patentee to commercially exploit the patent for a period of twenty years.

Patent: What?

The term 'Patent' comes from the latin word 'Patere' which means 'to lay open'.

A patent is an instrument granted by the government to provide certain rights and privileges known as patentee rights that enable inventor/patent holder to exploit the invention and in case of infringement(s), to approach the court for redressal.

Rationale underlying patenting

The rationale underlying patenting is synthesised as follows:

(1) To encourage scientific research, new technology and industrial progress.

(2) Grant of exclusive privilege to own/use/sell stimulates new inventions of commercial utility.

(3) The price of grant of monopoly is the disclosure of the invention. The disclosure can be utilised by other inventors to trigger further research and invention.

(4) The invention passes into the public domain after 20 years.

The grant of patent is done by the sovereign of a state to an inventor in exchange for full disclosure of the invention.

The patentee has the right to stop others from commercially exploiting the patented invention.

There is a lot of controversy regarding the benefits of patenting. The benefits of patenting ensue to all the stakeholders in patents and technological growth.

Benefits to the patent holder

- Recognition
- Commercial exploitation of the patent for 20 years.
- Patentee has the right to stop others from commercially exploiting his/her patent.
- Correlation of patents with organisational success. The number of patents that an organisation has generated is a leading indicator of its success in future.
- Legal protection to the patentee. In case the inventor does not patent it, then someone else in the know of the invention can patent the invention for himself.

- Protection from unfair competition.

Benefits to the Economy

- New products at cheaper prices
- New processes enhancing efficiency
- Springboard for research
- Easy system of technology transfer
- Trigger for more inventions
- Catalyses economic growth

Thus, patenting is a powerful system which needs to be leveraged by the inventor. In case the inventor chooses to ignore the patenting system, the inventor is likely to lose control over the invention and someone else would exploit it commercially at the expense of the inventor, resulting in considerable heartburn.

Subject Matter of Patents

Every new concept cannot be patented. Only inventions can be patented.

Then the question arises —'What is an invention'?

Invention means

(1) New Product/Process

(2) Involving an inventive step

(3) Capable of industrial application

Not every product or process innovation that we generate is capable of being patented. For it to be patentable it must satisfy two parameters:

- It should be new
- It must involve an 'Inventive Step'

Element of Newness: How do we determine that a product or process innovation that we have generated is new?

The newness or novelty means that the product or process innovation should not be a part of the "prior art" of the country. Prior art refers to existing knowledge, existing publication or existence in public use. Thus, the product or process innovation shall have novelty if it not a part of the DMP of the country in reference to the requisite product or process.

Element of 'Inventive Step'

The second parameter is that the product or process innovation should involve an inventive step.

'What is an inventive step?'

Inventive Step means that it should be non-obvious to a person skilled in the art.

If an ordinary skilled person can produce the same result then the inventive step is missing.

Contents of the Application for Patenting: Complete Specifications

(1) Title of the invention: Indicating subject matter of the invention.

(2) Drawings.

(3) Model: To be provided in case it is required by the Patent Controller. It is not a part of the specifications.

(4) Description of the invention.

(5) Operation of the invention and the best method of performing the invention.

(6) Scope of the invention

-Claims

-Claims that define the legal boundary of the invention.

(7) Technical Abstract.

Critical parameter for grant of a patent:A critical parameter for the grant of a patent is that the product or process should create enhanced efficacy in comparison to the existing products/processes.

Case:Patent for Spiriva, an asthma drug, revoked

Cipla, an Indian generic drugs manufacturing company successfully opposed the patent on Spiriva on the grounds that it lacked inventive step and that there was no enhancement in therapeutic efficacy.

Case: Patent on Glivec, an anti-cancer drug,

The patent on Glivec, an anti-cancer drug was revoked on the basis of the parameter that it did not demonstrate enhanced therapeutic efficacy.
A new form of a known substance that does not demonstrate enhanced efficacy is not patentable.

Case : Plastic Kilta

A device for manually hauling agricultural produce in hilly areas. The device is composed of a container of synthetic polymer material consisting of a hollow conical body open at the top and closed at the base, tapering from the operative open top to the base with perforated walls. The wall of the container has a contour adapted to proximate the back of a human body. The container also has a removable harness secured to it. The harness has straps and a buckle to secure the container to the individual. The looping is done around the back and shoulder of the individual. This can be adjusted to individuals with different heights and body structure. The traditional kilta was made of bamboo. The plastic kilta is made of polypropylene copolymer. The plastic kilta has detachable nylon straps and buckles.

Now the questions arise,

Q. Is this invention patentable? Why/Why not?

Q. Does it satisfy the key parameters of a patentable invention? Which parameters does it satisfy/not satisfy? Substantiate.

Q. Does it involve an inventive step? Substantiate?

Case : Wireless telephony receiving apparatus

Product Patent: Wireless telephony

At a receiving station, it is necessary to extract the waves of desired wavelength from the infinite number of waves that are reaching the antennae. This is achieved by the use of a tuned circuit containing a condenser. The condenser contains two sets of plats, one of which may be made moveable or variable with respect to the other, thus varying the capacity of the condenser and adjusting the resonant frequency so as to correspond to the frequency of the desired wave.

Description by the inventor:Selective tuning is secured by the use of a plurality of resonant circuits arranged to cascade in such a manner that the selectivity of the system increases in geometric ratio with the number of circuits employed. The selective circuits are respectively interlinked by a relay controlling a separate source of energy to initiate oscillations corresponding to potential oscillations impressed upon the relay. As each tuned circuit is more or less opaque to disturbing oscillations differing in frequency from the oscillations to be selected, a certain percentage of the disturbances is eliminated in each circuit of the series so that the purity of the incoming train of oscillations progressively increases as it is successively relayed. The relay preferably used for this purpose is an electron discharge tube having an incandescent cathode, an anode and a grid. The condenser on the input circuit, i.e. the circuit connected with the cathode of the electron discharge tube is indicated as being a variable condenser.

Prior Art:

Alexanderson's system when published was generally accepted and adopted in the art. Selectivity was apt to result in diminution of signal strength. This had been realised by others and certain devices had been suggested for overcoming it. For example, The employment of a relay in a mechanical or acoustic form by Lorenz. For this purpose Alexanderson suggests the use of the vacuum tube for coupling the several circuits together at each relay.

The vacuum tube which in Alexanderson's invention performs the function of keeping up the signal strength was not itself new. The prior publication was that of a German Patent. The main object of that invention was amplification and not selectivity. The condensers used in this patent as represented by the blueprint, were not variable.

Now to answer a few questions,

Q. Is Alexanderson's invention patentable?

Q. Is the invention novel? Does it have an inventive step?

Q. Anticipation of an invention destroys its patentability. Was Alexanderson's invention 'Anticipated'?

____

____

____

____

Q. What characteristics of the German Patent would have destroyed the novelty of Alexanderson's invention?

____

____

____

There is a significant overlap between the parameters that determine patentability of an invention and the innovator's framework. This indicates alignment between the innovator's framework and the patentability framework.

The patentability of an innovation is determined by its novelty,the presence of inventive step,whether the invention was anticipated and increased efficacy. If any of the aforementioned parameters is missing then the patent application is likely to be rejected or even if the patent is granted there is likelihood of a future challenge to the validity of the patent.

A disciplined implementation of the innovator's framework and the innovation development process would ensure that the innovator does not to face failure at the stage of patenting. However, patenting is limited to products and processes only.

End Note

Innovation is a necessary tool in the struggle for evolution at the institution or the individual level. It is very depressing to see individuals or institutions at the same level where they were years ago.

Why are they at the same level?

They are the same level because they failed to innovate.

Thus innovation is a critical competency for anyone who wants to grow, who cannot stand the status quo and who has not got into the habit of living with the problems and treating them as part of the context to such an extent that they are not visible anymore.

Innovation being a competency needs to be developed. It is a conscious competency. Hence,even if we have the potential to be innovators,the potential will never fructify unless a conscious effort is made.

Without conscious attention,the innovation potential will never convert and we shall be stuck in the process of endless repetition of what we already know. We shall never be in a position to push the boundaries of our knowledge and competency base and the best possible outcome shall be survival in a state of slow decline.

Conscious focus on innovation involves the identification of innovation hotspots, the utilisation of the innovator's framework, the innovation development process,innovation tools, levers, patent databases and the deployment of the innovation ecosystem.

These enable an institution or individual to generate innovations at a steady frequency of success thereby enabling the entity to transcend its limitations and achieve levels of success and effectiveness which were earlier considered impossible.